There

is an

Answer

Leith Samuel

Christian Focus Publications Ltd

Previously published by Victory Press

© 1990 Leith Samuel

ISBN 1 871676 06 1

Published by Christian Focus Publications Ltd

Christian Focus Publications is a non-denominational
publishing house.
The views expressed in our books are those of the authors.

Scripture quotations are from various versions. In some
instances, the author has paraphrased to make the meaning
clearer.

Contents

FOREWORD

We live in a society which is beset by problems. Of course, some of them derive from the complexity of modern life, but most of them are just the basic recurring problems of being human and living in a fallen world.

Sadly, that world is full of blind guides who are all too ready to offer specious answers to some of the deepest problems with which people wrestle. This is why this book is so important and so helpful.

All who have known Mr. Leith Samuel throughout his long and fruitful ministry recognise that he has an unusually sensitive pastor's heart. In a large city church in Southampton with a very cosmopolitan congregation, he has met all these problems at first-hand and has sought the ultimate answers in the wisdom of God in Scripture.

Here, he helps us to think them through in a way which is thoroughly practical, eminently sensible, and entirely Biblical.

It is a book for everyone to possess, and to pass on to others. That would be particularly true for pastors who will find this book invaluable. Mr. Samuel has put us all even further in his debt.

Eric Alexander.

Chapter 1

DOUBT

We have all met people who can boast, 'I have never had a day's illness in my life,' and others who can say concerning their Christian faith, 'I have never had a moment's doubt.' But most of us have had illness in one form or another, however mild compared with what some people have had to battle against. And many of us have had to fight against doubts. Sometimes it is during an illness that doubt gets a foothold in our mind. On the other hand, illness can make us realise our need of God and help us to commit our lives to Him.

But we don't have to be ill to doubt. You may be in perfect health and yet find yourself wondering at times whether there is a living God behind everything, after all. Can you remember how you felt when you saw the pictures of the Herald of Free Enterprise on its side near the Zeebrugge harbour? When you heard about the Chinook helicopter crashing near Aberdeen? The Piper Alpha oil rig tragedy in the same area? The Lockerbie plane crash? The King's Cross fire? The Clapham Junction accident? The Hillsborough football ground disaster? Has the powerful impact of all these disasters rocked your faith and disturbed your peace of mind?

How can a God who loves the creatures He has made allow such terrible things to happen, disaster after disaster? Do such tragedies make you wonder whether you can remain intellectually honest and still go on believing in the Christian faith? Or does your faith allow for such things without being rocked, no matter how deep your sympathy for the victims and their relatives?

Perhaps your thoughts have gone in another direction. If God can plan so vast a universe, create it and hold it in being – sun, moon and stars and all the space between for space-travellers to explore – how can He notice or care for an individual so small and insignificant as you or me? Do you doubt His personal interest in you? Or is yours the more basic doubt – how can He exist? How can there be an uncreated Creator, an uncaused Cause? The little girl who asked her mother, 'How can we be sure it is all true, Mummy? How can we be sure it isn't all a fairy story?' is not the only one wondering if Christian faith isn't all a myth, based on an imaginative story of the most delightful dimensions, the product of human dreaming and longing.

Perhaps you are shocked at reading such questions. You may feel that it is treason for a professing Christian to entertain thoughts like these. On the other hand, you may have been plagued by doubts that made it difficult for you to sustain your faith.

Let me say without a moment's hesitation that it is not enough to take a firm grip on ourselves and steel our wills to believe. Faith in God is not the product of human determination, or we could hardly expect to find believers outside the ranks of the strong-minded. 'I *must* believe or I'll be sunk,' does not bring a wavering Christian back to faith. And when the non-Christian says, 'I *must* have something to believe in, and it might as well be God as anything else,' it brings him nowhere near the Christian faith.

The answer to doubt is not 'I must *make* myself believe, somehow,' or 'At least I must try to believe.' *The answer to doubt is fact.* In this age that thinks so highly of psychology, far too many are trying to take to pieces their faith mechanism or ability-to-believe, instead of using it to make contact with the One whom God has sent for us to trust in. To trust someone is to put real faith in him, not just to believe *about* him. Anything that falls short of this personal trust falls short of real faith. To believe in the Lord Jesus Christ necessitates trusting myself to Him. If I have never personally trusted myself to Him I have never *really* believed *in* Him, no matter how many facts I may have believed *about* Him. The more facts I know about any person's trustworthiness, the more ground I have for trusting him.

This is true about God. He has revealed Himself. A countless multitude of facts point not only to His existence but to His unfailing trustworthiness. The truth may be known. We need not ask, despairingly, wistfully or contemptuously with Pilate, 'What is truth?' as if there were no answer to the question. The truth has been revealed to the world of men. But 'in their wickedness they are stifling the truth. For all that may be known of God by men lies plain before their eyes; indeed God Himself has disclosed it to them. His invisible attributes, that is to say His everlasting power and deity, have been visible, ever since the world began, to the eye of reason, in the things He has made. There is therefore no possible defence for their conduct; knowing God, they have refused to honour Him as God, or to render Him thanks. Hence all their thinking has ended in futility, and their misguided minds are plunged in darkness' (Rom. 1:18-21 N.E.B.)

The world of nature around us *should* convince us there is a God, but we are sadly blind to the message of its beauty. We are deaf to the message of the song of the birds and the rise and fall of the tide. We are insensitive to the message of the fragrant flowers, sea-breezes and mighty winds.

Neither rainbow nor sunset, flowers, birds nor scented shrubs can prove God's existence to us or bring us peace with God. Nor can the moral standards revealed in the Ten Commandments or in the Sermon on the Mount, though these should bring home to our consciences a sense of our personal need of God's forgiveness for past failure and His enabling strength for present circumstances.

The God the Christians worship cannot be located by any rocket. Astronomers cannot get Him on the end of their telescopes. Jodrell Bank cannot pick up the sound of His movements. Biologists cannot get a section of Him under their microscopes. Astronauts cannot shoot up the Milky Way to His front door, as it were. But an astronomer can, like Kepler, 'think God's thoughts after Him.' A biologist can have the Spirit of God living in his heart. An astronaut can sail through outer space with the Creator as his travelling companion – if he has found His transforming friendship, His forgiveness, His cleansing and His peace. We cannot find God by going up into the skies, for God is a Spirit. But God can indeed be found.

If we are looking for certainty about God we must turn our eyes upon the Lord Jesus Christ. Into this world of humanity, with its selfishness, lust and rebellion, has come the eternal Son of God. He came to deal with the greatest problem the world has ever known, which is not political, economic, military, educational or sociological. Our greatest problem is sin. When we look with unbiased mind at the modern scene it becomes quite clear that the selfishness of man, going his own way instead of God's way, is at the root of all our problems. And God has broken into history in the person of Jesus Christ to deal with this very thing. He was born in fulfilment of supernatural promise. Unlike us, He chose to be born. He chose His mother. He chose His birthplace. He chose an exceedingly humble environment. Unlike us, He never chose to sin, to assert His will against His Father's will, unfolded to Him day by day. But He did choose to die for our sins. He, the just, died on behalf of us, the unjust, that He might be able to take us by the hand and bring us to God. 'He suffered under Pontius Pilate.' This is a fact of history, from which we date our calendar. Even the periodicals which most blatantly deny the existence of God tacitly bear witness to His intervention in history by the date they bear. 'On the third day He rose again from the dead.' This is every bit as much a fact of history as any other. He has not died again. 'I am He that liveth, and was dead; and, behold, I am alive for evermore' (Rev. 1:18).

Christ's resurrection on the third day has been described by a leading lawyer of this century as 'one of the best attested facts of history'.* It is a fact of history that ever since that resurrection day Christians have worshipped Jesus Christ as Saviour and God, on the first day of the week. All over the world they were worshipping Him on the first day of this week. Were you among them?

It is a fact of history that seven weeks after Jesus Christ was crucified outside the walls of old Jerusalem no less than 3,000 men, Jews by birth or conversion, were baptised in His name, in the same city. They publicly confessed their faith in Him as the Son of God who died, was buried, on account of their sins, and who had risen from the dead, the Mighty Conqueror of sin, death and the grave.

It is a fact of history that the men who preached so effectively on that day of Pentecost were the very same men who had so recently forsaken Him and fled in fear. But were they *exactly* the same men? The coming of the Holy Spirit into their hearts had brought about a remarkable inward transformation. The cowards were now brave men. And this miracle of transformation still takes place today in the lives of men and women and boys and girls of every age group who commit their lives completely into the hands of the risen Christ.

It is a fact of history that Christian baptism can be traced back in an unbroken chain to the very time when people first became known as Christians.

It is a fact of history that the Lord's Supper, the breaking of bread and the drinking of wine, in remembrance of Christ's death, can be traced back in an unbroken chain to the time when He said to His disciples, 'Do this in remembrance of Me.'

I believe that one reason why our Lord instituted the Holy Communion was to revive drooping faith as well as to strengthen flagging love. Do you say, 'I wish there was something I could touch with my hands to assure me of the reality of these things?' There is something you can touch. There is the Bible, 'the most priceless treasure this world affords': there is also bread for you to touch and taste when you have trusted Christ, a cup for you to hold, wine for you to drink. Here are tangible links with what happened so long ago in history.

It is a fact of history that during the nineteen centuries since Christ walked on earth, things have happened in the hearts of men who have faced His claims. Wherever the Gospel, God's good news, has been proclaimed, some have scoffed, some have been vaguely interested, but others have turned from their sinful, selfish lives and put their trust in Him. Such lives have been changed from within by God's divine power.

> Something must have happened to free a sinner slave,
> Something must have happened to make a coward brave;
> 'Tis this, that Christ is risen, almighty now to save,
> And everyone who owns Him King finds something still is happening.

It is a fact, too, that the world situation today is remarkably like the picture Christ painted of the days which would precede His second coming to this world. He forewarned that there would be a great falling away from the faith, that people would get completely absorbed in the material things of this world, that the powers of the heavens would be shaken — and isn't that just how some would describe the mastery of outer space? He also spoke of men's hearts failing them for fear because of those things which were coming upon the earth. (See Luke 17: 26-33 and 21: 25-36.)

All these things are facts. And the answer to doubt is *fact*. Weigh up these things and see what a coherent picture they present. See the focal point. God has broken into history in sending His Son. He is going to send Him again to be the Judge of all men.

Sometimes smouldering doubts are fanned into flames by very personal situations. Some time ago, when there was more trouble in Cyprus than in Northern Ireland, a heart-broken mother asked me, 'How can there be a loving God when my son was allowed to die in that awful way?' She was troubled by facts, awful facts. Her problem arose from partial knowledge. She knew the facts about her son. She didn't know the facts about God's Son. The God in whom we trust, who commands all men everywhere to repent and to turn away from their selfish, sinful living, is the God who sent His Son to a troubled land not far from Cyprus. There He died the most awful death.

What had He done to deserve it? Nothing. He was the only sinless Man the world has ever seen. But the sin of the world gathered upon His great heart of love; and that heart was broken under the weight of it. He who knew no sin was made sin for us, 'that we might be made the righteousness of God in Him' (II Cor. 5:21). Something unspeakably awful happened to Him so that something unspeakably wonderful might happen to us. Hearing these *facts* opened the eyes of the troubled mother. She could no longer argue that a loving God would not allow such a thing to happen. A loving God had loved her so much that He had allowed a worse thing to happen – for her sake. She saw this. Her fighting against God ceased. She no longer doubted His love or His power. 'Lord, I believe: help Thou my unbelief,' was her prayer. If you have a tragedy, have you brought it to Calvary, where the blackness of what has happened to us pales into something much less intense in the light of the sufferings of the Son of God? Under the shadow of His agony we may find relief from ours.

Let me close on a positive note. The answer to doubt is fact. And the opposite of doubt is faith. And 'faith cometh by hearing and hearing by the word of God' (Rom. 10:17). This is why John says towards the end of his Gospel record of the facts of Christ's life-work and teaching, death and resurrection, 'There are many other signs (evidences of the justness of His claims and the reality of His resurrection) which Jesus did in the presence of His disciples which are not written in this book: but these things are written that you may believe (i.e. to bring you to faith, to deliver you from your doubts) that Jesus is the Christ, the Son of God; and that believing you might have life through His name.' (See John 20:30-31.)

There are no worse doubts than doubts about the person and work of Christ. Will you turn to John's Gospel and read it carefully – eternity is at stake – asking God to bring home to your understanding and conscience the facts about Christ, so that you may come to put your trust in Him as your Saviour. If you are persuaded already that Jesus Christ is the Son of God, the Saviour you need, but you have been doubting whether He would have anything to do with you, whether He could meet your need, make you whole and useful to Him, doubt no longer. He says, 'Come unto Me, all you who labour and are heavy laden, and I will give you rest.' (See Matt. 11:28-30 and compare John 6:37.) Trust yourself to Him for the forgiveness of all your sins and cleansing from all their stains. Trust Him to put His Spirit inside your innermost being. Trust Him to take your life and make you all He wants you to be. A vital, personal faith in a living, personal Saviour will bring you out of the shadows of doubt and keep you from the cliffs of despair. 'Happy are they who never saw Me and yet have found faith' (John 20:29 N.E.B.).

* See *The Evidence for the Resurrection*, Prof. J.N.D. Anderson of London University. I.V.P.

Chapter 2
SUFFERING

FACING THE PROBLEM

'I would like to believe in God,' he said, with obvious sincerity, 'but the thought of all the suffering in the world makes it very difficult for me to believe in a God of love. Surely, if there is a good God He is all-powerful and could stop it. Why does He seem to stand by and do absolutely nothing?'

There is no doubt that the problem of suffering is one of the greatest stumbling blocks to faith and is a difficulty sooner or later to nearly everyone who thinks seriously about God.

There are, of course, many kinds and causes of suffering, and not all suffering is of the same intensity. Purely physical pain is sometimes the easiest kind to bear. Misunderstanding or mental cruelty may have much deeper effects and be much harder to endure. 'Man's inhumanity to man' is a frequent cause of suffering. This may be on a vast scale, as when six million Jews were gassed and burned or exterminated by other equally callous means at the hands of the Nazis. Or it may be on a smaller scale, such as the petty cruelty of one individual to another turning someone's life into a hell on earth.

Human selfishness and lust account for much of the suffering in the world, as in the bitterness of racial strife, the unhappiness of broken homes or the rising incidence of venereal disease among young people, which is causing so much concern to medical health authorities just now.

And human ignorance can cause suffering, too, as seen in the tragic effects of an unproved tranquilliser in the birth of thalidomide babies.

Once we stop to think, however, we begin to realise how much human suffering is avoidable. No one has any right to blame God when a drunken driver causes loss of life and limb, or when a heavy cigarette smoker dies in great discomfort of lung cancer.

But there are tragedies which have no visible human cause, e.g. in consequence of earthquakes, floods, volcanic eruption, lightning. Even some of these tragedies, however, could be avoided, for sheltering underneath a tree during a storm or building a house near a volcano or on low ground near a river known to rise dangerously at times is asking for trouble.

But the fact is that we all know of terrible personal tragedies which have made us wonder why they are allowed to occur or build up to their climax. We have to admit that we do not know why God allows these things. Could it be that God allows them because He can use them as a warning to a careless world (Ps. 50:1,2)? And it is not wrong to question why, so long as we do not ask it in bitterness.

'Why does God allow...?' is no problem to the man who has no desire to believe in God. An atheist cannot reasonably ask why God allows suffering. To him, there is no God to allow it or to stop it! To him, there is no Creator to give the initial impetus to life, no Heavenly Father to care for His children in their suffering, no eternal Judge to vindicate the innocent, to reward the righteous and punish the wicked, no living Christ seeking to bring men into personal communion with Himself. In fact, as Professor C.S. Lewis points out, the unbeliever might as well ask however Christians came to believe in a God of love at all when there is so much suffering in the world! So let us look at the problem of suffering from the Christian's point of view.

Christians believe:

There is a living God, who created all things well.
Man, His creature, was designed to live in joyful
harmony with his Creator and with his fellow men.
God is wise and loving.
God is omnipotent (all-powerful).

Yet it is this very teaching which raises the problem
in its most acute form. Surely, if God is loving He
would want to stop human suffering. If He is powerful
He would be able to stop it. If He is wise he would
know how to stop it. Therefore, by the rules of logic it
would seem He cannot be all three – loving, powerful
and wise! But Christianity claims He is all three at
once. He loves the man who suffers, He is completely
able to stop the suffering, and His wisdom knows how
and when to do so – and yet the suffering continues.
Why?

FREE WILL

This problem of suffering has troubled the minds of
men since the dawn of human history, and there is no
slick, easy answer. But the Bible has some wonderful
clues.

Right at the beginning of the Bible we find God
giving man freedom of choice. Had Adam not been
given free-will there would have been no human
suffering.

Perhaps you are thinking, 'Why didn't God make
man fool-proof, incapable of sinning?' Because God
wanted men who could choose to love Him, choose the
right from the wrong, men who could make rational
choices, men who would weave on earth a character
they would wear through eternity. 'But since God knew
the world was going to get into such a shocking mess,
isn't God responsible for giving men a capacity they
might abuse?' Yes, we may reverently say God is

responsible for this gift and, for His part, He has accepted His responsibility, and we shall consider (further on) how He has met it to the full in Christ.

But have you ever thought what we would be like if we had been made without free-will? Without free-will, man would have neither the need nor the ability to make decisions. His conscience, which tells him, 'Don't do this...don't do that...you ought to have done that...' would be unnecessary if he were fool-proof. The emotions play their part in human decisions. These would be reduced to an instinct. He would have an enforced affinity with what he ought to love and resistless apathy towards what he ought to hate. If the capacities of judgement, conscience and emotion are removed there is little point in man having understanding either! What is left is scarcely human! We have a quasi-human robot, a fool-proof machine perhaps, but not a man.

The Bible teaches that man is made in the image of God with the threefold capacity to love, to will and to think. God made man capable of choosing and responsible for his choices, his decisions and his actions. The sufferings which may follow are an integral part of this glorious fact that we were made not robots but in God's image. It is on the anvil of daily routine and difficult circumstances that Christian character is hammered out for those who realise that God is after something precious with every pressure He allows to come into our lives. We may be sure that He never allows us to suffer any temptations or trials beyond our powers of endurance. He always sees to it that there is a way out. (See 1 Cor. 10:13 and Jude 24,25.)

THE FALL OF MAN

But we must be clear as to what we mean when we say the Bible teaches that man was made in the image of

God. For the Bible teaches equally clearly that the image of God in man was marred very soon after his creation. (See Gen. 3:22; 4:8; 5:3.) The fall of man has left its spoiling mark on the whole of humanity ever since. When the woman was deceived into disobedience and the man sided with her, the creature, instead of with his Creator, his disobedience entered into the fibre of his being. And man has been basically in revolt against his Maker ever since.

Because man's free-will was abused, by being used for his own immediate satisfaction rather than for God's glory, every moral capacity he had was affected. Human nature lost its original perfect freedom to communicate with the Creator and to do His will. It is this warped human nature that we all inherit.

You and I were not born with totally free will, morally or spiritually neutral; we were born spiritually dead, completely off God's wave-length, without natural desire to please Him and morally inclined to sin and every form of self-indulgence rather than righteousness. The fear of AIDS, syphilis, and gonorrhea keeps many from promiscuity who have little respect for a woman's personality.

The theologians speak of 'total depravity'. This does not mean that everybody is in every respect utterly depraved. It means that every capacity, thought, will, affection, imagination is 'out of line'. And we all suffer in consequence, to a greater or lesser degree.

Is it any wonder, in the light of this, that Jesus said to Nicodemus, 'You must be born again'? Patching up human nature will not do. A new creation is needed. This calls for nothing less than a miracle, a creative act of God in the human heart. Paul speaks of a Christian as one whose new nature is 'being renewed in knowledge after the image of its Creator' (John 3:1-16; II Cor. 5:17-21; Col. 3:10 R.S.V.).

SUFFERING AND SIN

For our next clue, within the limited confines of this
chapter, we turn to the book of Job. The statement that
human suffering is due to human sin is not to be
understood as meaning that everyone's suffering is in
exact proportion to his own sin. Job's friends, known
somewhat ironically as 'comforters', made that mis-
take, reflecting the theological prejudices of all their
fellow Jews. 'If any man is suffering, he must have
sinned in some special way. And your particular
suffering must be due to some terrible sin.' But they
were wrong. Job insisted that they were wrong. God
showed Job his need for repentance despite his outward righteousness, but vindicated his main argument
against his friends. Job's sufferings were to purify and
strengthen his faith, not to purge and atone for his sins.
(See Job and Heb. 12:1-14.)

Although the causes of some suffering are clear to be
seen, we must not try to blame ourselves, or others, for
everything that goes wrong. Let us rather seek to learn
all the lessons we can through our trouble and ask God
to refine our characters when we pass through the fires
of suffering. As Christians, our attitude to personal
suffering should be governed by this, that the only
completely innocent Man the world has ever known,
the spotless Son of God, suffered more than any other
man before or since in the physical, mental and
spiritual pain which He endured on behalf of the
creatures He had made.

REDEMPTIVE SUFFERING

And His suffering had a wonderful purpose. The Bible
says, 'Christ has once suffered, (He) the righteous for
(us) the unrighteous, that He might bring us to God.'
(See I Pet. 3:18.) It was through sin that both suffering

and death entered human experience. (See Rom. 5:12-21.) Christ came to suffer the judgement due to sin, so that all who believe in Him might be freed from condemnation and the pains of everlasting suffering in the life of the world to come.

'Why does God allow suffering?' seems to pale into insignificance alongside the question, 'Why did God allow His Son to suffer like that?' And the answer to this second question is simply, 'for us men and for our salvation'. Through His suffering, He purged a world's guilt. The greatest thing God has ever done for humanity He has done through suffering. And none who believe in Him can dare to ask *as if there were no answer*, 'Why does God allow suffering?'

OUR OWN ATTITUDE

The New Testament does not stop at the redemptive sufferings of the Son of God. It deals with the sufferings of ordinary human beings like ourselves. Romans 8 speaks of the temporary nature of suffering for the believer, the glories that await him and the final deliverance of human creation from the frustrations of this life. Peter's First Letter speaks in every chapter of suffering which strengthens people who choose to suffer rather than to deny their faith. They are to know joy even in their suffering on earth here and now, as well as deliverance from it hereafter. The God who allows the suffering is the God who sends the joy.

He give us more grace when the burdens grow greater;
He sends us more strength when the labours increase;
To added affliction, He adds still more mercy,
To multiplied trials His multiplied peace.

Then there is that magnificent passage, (II Cor. 4:16-18,) which gives one of the clearest insights into why God allows suffering in the lives of His own faithful people. Here we find encouragement not to lose heart in tough and painful circumstances, but to look ahead to the fruit in eternity that is being produced by the right attitude to our present suffering. God always makes our troubles work for our ultimate good. (See Rom. 8:28.)

Our natural tendency is to consider as good the things that make for our comfort and ease in this life. But God *puts character before comfort.* To whom do we turn instinctively in time of trouble? To someone who has always had an easy life, or to someone who has weathered some of life's storms and who therefore can bring us that wonderful human quality known as sympathy?

We are not intended to go to the extreme of seeking suffering for the sake of the refinement it may bring to our character! God will order our circumstances in His own way, if we trust our lives to Him. The light and the shadow, the sunshine and the storms, are all part of our life on earth.

Thy way, not mine, O Lord,
However dark it be;
Lead me by Thine own hand,
Choose Thou the path for me.

Just as the most valuable steel is tempered in fire and the strongest trees can develop their deep roots through storms, so the mystery of suffering produces greatness of character in those who accept it aright. 'The sufferings of this present time are not worth comparing with the glory that is to be revealed to us and in us.' Or, as J.B. Phillips translates the Apostle Paul's Letter to the Romans chapter 8:18-23, 'In my opinion whatever we may have to go through now is less than nothing compared with the magnificent future God has planned for us...The world of creation cannot as yet see Reality, not because it chooses to be blind, but because in God's purpose it has been so limited — yet it has been given hope. And the hope is that in the end the whole of created life will be rescued from the tyranny of change and decay, and have its share in that magnificent liberty which can only belong to the children of God! It is plain to anyone with eyes to see that at the present time all created life groans in a sort of universal travail. And it is plain, too, that we who have a foretaste of the Spirit are in a state of painful tension, while we wait for that redemption of our bodies...'

Not till the loom is silent,
And the shuttles cease to fly,
Will God unroll the canvas
And explain the reason why
The dark threads are as needful
In the weaver's skilful hand
As the threads of gold and silver
For the pattern He has planned.

You may remember that when the Lord Jesus had washed Simon Peter's feet, just after the last supper on the night on which He was betrayed, He said to him, 'What I am doing you do not know now, but afterward you will understand.' I do not think we are stretching the meaning of the words too far when we understand Him to include what He allows to come into the life of His child as well as what He actively performs. His loving wisdom and sovereign over-ruling cover every circumstance of the Christian's life.

This thought is a great help to many Christians when faced afresh, as many of us often are, with the question we have been considering. If we knew as much as God knows, and had His wisdom, His love and His power, we would arrange and allow things exactly as He does. One day we will know why!

Meantime, those of us who have proved God's love to us in Christ, and know the deep peace that follows His forgiveness, have good reason for deliberately trusting His wisdom, where we cannot knowingly trace or understand His ways. He who spared not His own Son but gave Him up (to death, and such a death at that) for us all — can we not trust such a God to give us, with Him, everything else that we can need? This giving includes the faith with which to go on trusting, patience till we reach the end of the tunnel and a happy issue out of all afflictions in His good time. And no matter what may happen, God's love will never fail.

Recommended for further reading on this subject:
Why do the innocent suffer? John Stott. Crusade reprint.
The Problem of Pain, C.S. Lewis, Fontana.
The Mystery of Suffering, H.A.E. Hopkins. I.V.F.
Your Suffering, Maurice Wood. Hodder.
Not by Chance: Making Sense out of Suffering, Brian Edwards. Evangelical Press.

Chapter 3

FEAR

What are you afraid of? Are you afraid of losing the person who means most to you in the world? Are you afraid of some particular illness? Are you afraid of dying or death? Is there some crash you are living in fear of?

I meet people suffering from all these forms of fear. These fears may be your fears. The Psalmist had his fears. He was afraid of going out of his mind. He was afraid of being handed back to his enemies in the land of his birth. He was afraid God might leave him to his own devices.

I am not exaggerating when I say that there are very few people who are not conscious at this time of fear in one form or another. Are you afraid of messing up your whole life through some foolish action or ignorance? The fear of making a mess of their own lives and dragging others down in their failure haunts many today. Are you afraid you will never shake off the grip of some sin? Do you fear you will never find forgiveness and peace of mind? Do you feel the helpless victim of circumstances?

The deepest fear to many is the fear of the unknown future. This crystallises in some minds round the fear of the destruction of the world or surviving as a maimed person in a partially destroyed world. In others in revolves round the fear of their marriage breaking down and their home breaking up. Some dread bereavement; others unemployment, poverty and starvation. Some fear being left on the shelf, battling through life alone; others are worried stiff about the folk at home, far away. These are some of our modern fears. Every fresh discovery, every new scientific conquest, while opening up new horizons, stirring up new hope and imparting a fresh sense of achievement, brings its own crop of new fears or fans into flame some of the old fears.

Perhaps you, too, are afraid of going out of your mind. There are so many mentally and nervously overwrought that the thing they fear most is becoming mentally unbalanced. How many times have you felt recently, 'I can't stand any more. This is the end'? Yet you have come up again. But you know of those who have cracked. And you are haunted by the fear that you may be the next to find 'something going snap inside you'.

The Psalmist says, 'I sought the Lord, and He heard me, and delivered me from all my fears' (Ps. 34:4). But it is such a far cry back to the simple living of the days of David that someone may say, 'His ideas were all right for that sort of civilisation, when men felt that God was near them. But look how far back we have pushed His frontiers now! Is it any use seeking the Lord today? Is He near enough? Is He big enough to stand up to our modern world? Can He handle our complex situations? Will He hear us as He heard David? Or, to be more personal, can He deliver *me* from *my* fears?' The answer to these questions is an unhesitating 'Yes'.

We are probing outer space with our brilliantly conceived instruments, but God is no more embarrassed by their presence than He is in difficulties over the movements of the myriads of bodies in orbit. He arranged for them millions of years ago. Atheists may boast, 'We have been up to see, and He is not there,' but who said God was *there*? We don't find God encouraging us to *go up* and search for Him in the heavens. And we may find Him without embarking on any journey into space.

And, what is more, there is an urgent message from

God to us. God is looking for us. God has *come down* to us. 'For God so loved the world, that He gave His only begotten Son,' – gave Him to a manger for a cradle and a cross for a throne – 'that whosoever believeth in Him should not perish, but have everlasting life' (John 3:16). 'God was in Christ, reconciling the world unto Himself,' dying on that cross outside the walls of old Jerusalem, 'not putting their trespasses down to their account...' Christ has come to seek and save the lost, the fearful, the broken-hearted. He can do for us what we cannot do for ourselves. He can make us whole. God is waiting to pour His grace upon *you*. You need no longer live in fear, if only you will turn from your sin to the Christ who died for your sin, trust yourself to Him as your Saviour and go out and obey Him. A doctor once said to me, 'I can't find peace of mind.' He had never come as a sinner needing God's forgiveness and pleading Christ's death for sinners. When he did, he found peace – peace which the world can neither give nor take away. He sought the Lord, and He heard him and delivered him from all his fears.

The living God has not only sent His Son to be our Saviour; He has sent His Holy Spirit, who has come to do a great work in the hearts and lives of those who believe in Christ. He is the Spirit of Love, and He releases something of God's own love inside our hearts. It is His perfect love that casts out fear. 'For God hath not given us the spirit of fear; but of power, and of love, and of a sound mind' (II Tim. 1:7). He 'delivered me from all my fears'.

Someone may be saying, 'It is all very well for you who were brought up in the Christian faith and have never had any doubts about it. What about the rest of us, confused by rival claims and troubled by a thousand doubts?' Let me remind you of the great invitation issued by the Lord Jesus, 'Come unto Me, all you who labour and are heavy laden, and I will give you rest'

(Matt. 11:28). He did not say, 'Those who are labouring under anything but *doubt!*' He said, 'all you who labour.' Bring Him your doubts and fears. It is not a great faith in a small Saviour that brings deliverance from our sins and our fears, but what little faith we have, placed in a great and wonderful Saviour.

Do you say, 'If only I could have more faith!'? You could have. 'Faith comes by hearing, and hearing by the word of God' (Rom. 10:17). Do you read the Bible? If not, why not start reading today? The more we read the Bible, the more we see how trustworthy Jesus Christ is. He is faithful. Others may go back on their word, but Christ never breaks His promises. And the more trustworthy we see Him to be, the more natural it is for us to put our trust in Him. He has promised, 'Him who comes to Me I will in no wise cast out' (John 6:37). He receives sinners. He cleanses them from their sins. He makes them new. He will receive you if you come to Him for cleansing and renewal.

Perhaps you have not been troubled by the fear of ultimate condemnation, the fear of never finding forgiveness. Perhaps what worries you is some habit you have formed, and you fear you will never be free in this life. Christians sing, 'He breaks the power of cancelled sin, He sets the prisoner free,' and this is the sober truth. He saves His people from their *sins,* not only from their condemnation. 'If the Son shall make you free, ye shall be free indeed' (John 8:36). He frees us for His own service. 'I sought the Lord, and He heard me, and delivered me from all my fears.'

One spring day I was standing on a balcony in Berkeley, California. Gleaming in the distance was 'The Bridge of the Golden Gate'. The building of this bridge got terribly behind schedule because there were so many casualties, and the men were scared of falling off. A huge safety net was placed beneath the area of operations. But this made no difference for a time. Still the work dragged. Then a riveter fell off, into the net. When he came up smiling, the men knew they were safe, and from that moment the project leapt ahead. If we trust ourselves to Christ He will give us true security, freedom from the fear of being lost, so that we can concentrate all our energies on serving Him. Christians are not toiling to save their souls. They are working for the One who has seen to all that for them. Bring Him the sin that is getting you down and the fears that haunt you, and ask Him to deliver you from them. He *will* set you free, free to serve Him. And His service is perfect freedom. 'I sought the Lord, and He heard me, and delivered me from all my fears.'

But maybe it is 'the future all unknown' that is troubling you. You are afraid of what is going to happen to you and your little ones. Don't panic! God is still on the throne. He is supreme, exercising His sovereignty over the affairs of the nations. Modern scientists are only discovering what He has uncovered. He has got the whole world in His hand and is working out His own purpose as year succeeds to year. One day, history, as we know it, will be wound up by its Creator. But that is not the end for the believer. 'Let not your hearts be troubled...In My Father's house are many mansions: if it were not so, I would have told you. I go to prepare a place for you. And if I go and prepare a place for you, I will come again, and receive you unto Myself; that where I am, there you may be also' (John 14:1-3). And until that day dawns, He has made precise plans and perfect provision for us and for our loved ones, whatever the days between may bring. 'I sought the Lord, and He heard me, and delivered me from all my fears.'

Will you not put your unknown future into the hands of Him who knows it perfectly? The future is as clear to Him as the past.

If you put yourself in His hands He will make you

what you ought to be. And no matter how tangled things are at the moment, He will sort them all out in His own time and way. He will heal your troubled mind. He will set you free from the grip of sin and guide you day by day through this troubled world.

Seek the Lord now, while He may be found. And you will be able to say as truthfully as David, 'I sought the Lord, and He heard me, and delivered me from all my fears.' 'The same Lord over all is rich unto all that call upon Him,' whatever their colour, background, country or upbringing. And 'whosoever shall call upon the name of the Lord shall be saved' (Rom. 10:12,13).

Bring Him your sorrows, bring Him your fears,
Bring Him your heartaches, bring Him your tears;
Come, tell Him plainly just how you feel:
Jesus will pardon, Jesus will heal.

Chapter 4

LONELINESS

THE PLIGHT OF THE LONELY

'Most people go through life in a coffin of loneliness,' said one of the interviewers in a B.B.C. programme. Was he exaggerating? I don't think so. He was just stating what is obvious to most social workers. Loneliness is one of the diseases of modern society.

Most of us have no idea at all about the loneliness many people experience. I know of some who live in the midst of bustling activity, surrounded with people; yet they are terribly lonely. I know others who live alone and yet are never lonely. They can say with the apostle Paul: 'I have learned, in whatsoever state I am, to be content.'

Circumstances influence all of us, but it is not the things around us, or the things that happen to us, that determine our fate. It is our attitude to those things that is the deciding factor. Some people are overwhelmed by tiny obstacles; others ride buoyantly over the most mountainous difficulty.

What is loneliness? It is a sense of unsatisfied desire. The lonely long for companionship, for friendship on an active basis. They long for that sense of completion and security that comes to those who feel they are wanted and cared for by others. They long to have contact with people without feeling that they are being a nuisance or getting in the way. They long to feel that they are really doing something useful, that they would be missed if they were not there.

What is the answer to loneliness? There are those to whom I have already referred who, living alone, are never lonely. These brave spirits have not achieved their happiness merely by the gift of nature. It is not just their temperament that makes them happy. The only adequate explanation of their condition is their relationship with an unseen Companion, who loves them with an everlasting love. They have discovered

THE MOST IMPORTANT FACTOR IN SOLVING THE PROBLEM

A friend who is really understanding, sympathetic, invigorating, who can see me more clearly than I can see myself, and bring me out of my shell, is my greatest need if my trouble is loneliness. And there is such a Friend, a Friend whose ear is open and whose arms are outstretched to the lonely. 'There is a friend who sticks closer than a brother' (Prov. 18:24). And His Name? Jesus. Children are expressing a wonderful truth when they sing:

The best Friend to have is Jesus:
He will hear me when I call;
He will keep me lest I fall;
Oh, the best Friend to have is Jesus.

But I cannot have Him as my Friend unless I am prepared to receive Him as my Saviour. Have you ever noticed that the well-known 'Shepherd Psalm' (the 23rd) follows the most vivid description of what happens to someone who is being crucified? – Psalm 22. If we would know the Shepherd's company and leading we must have the Saviour's forgiveness and cleansing. For it is the Saviour who brings us out of our coffins of sin and self-centredness. He raises us from spiritual death. He brings us out of the darkness and the valley of the shadow. He takes the sting out of physical death. When we turn to Him the dawn of eternal day is upon us. The oppressive blanket of loneliness can cut us off no more. Life begins to have new meaning, however disappointed, weak or old we may be. Life begins to add up and make sense.

He is an unchanging Friend. He is the perfect Friend. He knows the worst about us and loves us just the same. He is the transforming Friend, ever finding ways and means of lifting us from our naturally low level of living to breathe the air of the higher ground that is equally natural to Him.

Those who find the Lord Jesus may have their moments of loneliness, just as they will have their moments of failure when they take their eyes off Him and look at themselves instead. But they can never have the same desolate sense of loneliness and forsakenness that many people who don't know the Saviour experience today.

'It is wonderful to know that I am no longer alone,' wrote a middle-aged person to me, a few days after she had trusted herself to the Lord Jesus. He is living in her heart. How can she be alone? As the Irishman said, 'When there's one of us now, there's always two of us.'

'Do you ever feel lonely?' I asked a man of eighty-five, bedridden for the past two years. He had some difficulty in getting his breath, but his eyes sparkled as he looked first at his wife and then at me and said, 'Lonely? How could I be lonely? He is always with me.' All Christians can count on His never-failing Presence. He has said (to those who trust Him as Saviour): 'I will never leave you, nor forsake you. So that we may boldly say, The Lord is my helper, and I will not fear what man shall do unto me' (Heb. 13:5,6). And He is the same yesterday, today and for ever.

WHAT THE LONELY CAN DO FOR THEMSELVES

Suggestions for those who are housebound

Leave an empty chair by your bed for Him. Leave an empty chair by the fireside for Him. Learn to speak naturally to Him as if you could see Him sitting in that chair. He is nearer than if He were. We don't need to use a special tone of voice or a special vocabulary to be heard by Him. He hears our faintest whisper. 'Practising the Presence of Christ' is what Brother Lawrence used to call it. Many real Christians in this restless age know all too little of this secret.

Listen to His voice when you read your Bible. The postman may pass your door without pausing, and you may feel, 'Forsaken again: nobody cares!' But if you read your Bible every day God will surely speak to you and make the Book live to you. His personal messages come day by day, with freshness and force, even to people who are familiar with exactly where each word is to be found on each page, after reading for years and years. Remember, too, by the way, that the person who receives letters is the one who writes them! Look out for someone else who longs for letters, and write to him or her.

Use your days of quietness

Do you remember the days when you were so busy that you hadn't much time for reading or unhurried prayer and meditation? Now, perhaps, time hangs on your hands. Use that time in prayer. Pray for your loved ones, your neighbours, your minister, the Christian workers in your church and town. Some people make a scrapbook with photographs of the people they are praying for; it helps them to visualise needs and to concentrate.

Ask God for some special assignment. Adopt some 'problem situations' you hear of, and pray them through. You cannot feel lonely while your mind is peopled with others and their needs. Ask your minister (or doctor) if there are any special needs for prayer, any information they can trust you with without betraying confidences, so that you may get behind them more intelligently in prayer. 'More things are wrought by prayer than this world dreams of.' To pray is to work.

Ask God to burden you with some of the missionaries on the field today and 'adopt' one or two of them. Pray systematically for them. Use their prayer-letters in your daily devotions as part of your own 'prayer-list'. Keep in touch with them. The most isolated Christian in the homeland can bring encouragement and joy to a missionary in a far, wearying country, just by writing the simplest of news and assurances of prayerful remembrance. They may not be able to write back very often, but you can be sure your loving remembrance is deeply appreciated. A world map on a piece of board, with photographs of special missionary links round the margin of the map, and with a red thread going from the picture to the missionary location, has helped many to pray through the day, as well as being a never-failing point of interest for visitors. If you are able to type, pray that God will lead you to a missionary recruit whose prayer-letter you can duplicate. If you have the time and energy to circulate it as well you will be in touch with a host of new friends whose gratitude will go out to you for the service you are doing for their friend, even if they do not often write to express their feelings.

Become a Prayer Companion to some missionary (e.g. through Overseas Missionary Fellowship or one of the Faith Missions which has such a scheme). This will give you more information and responsibility than the usual prayer partnership. Read missionary biographies, such as Hudson Taylor, J.O. Fraser, C.T. Studd, Amy Carmichael, Isobel Kuhn, and fill the rooms of memory and imagination with the fragrance of those lives. Thus your interest in prayer will be deepened, and you will get to know these folk through the printed page before you have the privilege of meeting them in heaven.

If you haven't the mental energy to do much reading, take hold of some promise from God's Word and meditate upon it; turn it into prayer, turn it into praise. An old saint I knew learned certain portions which had been extra helpful to him through his Christian life, and he used to recite a different one each day of the week and ponder its truths. He spent many months in bed before the Saviour called him home, and these 'exceeding great and precious promises', statements and exhortations helped to keep loneliness far from him.

Madame Guyon was more than 'housebound'. She was a prisoner in the Bastille because of her Christian faith. A narrow slit in the nine-foot-thick walls let in what light there was. Her cell was dreary and cold in the winter and suffocating in the summer. She was allowed no books, no recreation, no tasks to occupy her mind. Yet in these circumstances she was able to scratch on the wall:

My cage confines me round:
Abroad I cannot fly;
But though my wings are closely bound
My heart's at liberty.
My prison walls cannot control
The flight, the freedom of the soul,
And in God's mighty will I find
The joy, the freedom of the mind.

Suggestions for those who are still active

If you are able to get about, and still have the energy to
go upstairs to a child that calls, you could bring great
joy to a young married couple by baby-sitting for them
so that they can get to a service or meeting together. A
number of young marrieds have to take it in turns to
attend a church service. What a thrill it would be for
them if occasionally they could go together! You can't
be lonely while doing such service, even though you
may feel a little strange in someone else's home to
start with.

Remember, too, that many elderly folk are housebound. A visitor makes the world of difference to
them. Some flowers from your garden will give them
a fragrant touch from the outside world. A little fruit
shared with them in the name of the Lord Jesus will
give them a new appetite for what may have become a
pretty monotonous diet. Even a meal prepared from
their own kitchen will taste different if served by
somebody else's hands. And your loneliness is
swallowed up in dispelling that of somebody else.

If you are able to entertain, invite to your home
people who look as lonely as you have felt. Stretch out
a friendly hand and you will find that sowing bountifully always leads to reaping bountifully. If you live in
rooms you will not be able to do much entertaining, but
you could add your name to the church's Sunday
luncheon rota. If your church has no such arrangement,
why not suggest it to the minister? It has made such a
difference to a Sunday, for strangers, where such a rota
is in action.

The Bible says, 'A man who would have friends must
show himself friendly.' Don't wait for someone to
befriend you; do the befriending yourself. The folk
around you may have misunderstood. They may have
been thinking you could not bear company at any price.

A smile goes a long way and costs so little. You can smile when you can't say a word. A stranger in church will be drawn back to that church if people smile at him instead of ignoring him, because they don't know him, or looking at him as if to say, 'Where on earth have you sprung from?' A friendly word after a service has led to that one finding Christ.

If you have no children of your own, or if yours have grown up and gone away, 'adopt' for regular prayer and watchful interest one or more of the young people in your church. So many temptations, some subtle, some blatant, assail young people today that there cannot be too much insulation of prayer and godly love surrounding them. Pray that desire for security and gain may not be the controlling factor in their lives. Pray that they may not get entangled with any life-partner other than the one of God's choice. Pray that they may have patience and discernment and steadfast loyalty to Jesus, an uncompromising witness and a genuine willingness to go anywhere the Lord may send them and to be what He would have them be.

Make friends with regular contacts, such as milkmen or postmen who call at your door. To find out their names and call them by them helps them to know that they matter to you personally and that your interest is not just in the things they bring round. They won't want to be kept talking for long or they won't get through their rounds. But they will be glad to know there is somebody who is interested in them as persons, someone to whom they can go when they are in trouble. They will be quite glad to receive an occasional Christian booklet from you. In this way, more than one regular caller has been won to Christ in time of need.

If loneliness is thrust on you for your uncompromising loyalty to the Lord Jesus and His standards (more than one Christian has been 'sent to Coventry' for refusing to 'fiddle' his time-sheet), disarm the bitterness of your critics by your gracious persistence in a cheery greeting. Picture them as the people they will be when some of them find the Saviour. If you suffer for doing the right thing there is always a blessing in it for you — and others — somewhere.

If you are young, (and the worst thing about loneliness is the fear of being left on the shelf for life,) resist the temptation to look on unmarried life as inevitably 'second best'. Far better to go through life alone than to be tied to the wrong life-partner. Some who, without much concern for God's will, succeed in getting a partner are far more lonely than many a single person happily engaged in daily work and 'outside activity'. If the will of God is that you should be single, in that course of life lies your true happiness. But if you are 'still hoping against hope', ask God if it is His will to keep the partner for you, to prepare you for your helpmate and to give you the patience to wait for His time. 'As for God, His way is perfect' (II Sam. 22:31). 'No good thing will He withhold from them that walk uprightly' (Ps. 84:11).

IN CONCLUSION

I appreciate that every reader who has been battling against loneliness will not be able to put into effect every one of the suggestions I have made. But it may be that one of them is the very thing for you. If so, don't just think about taking action one day; do something about it soon. Loneliness is among the testings which assail all sorts and conditions of men. And just as no testing has overtaken you save such as is common to man, so God is faithful, who will not suffer you to be tested beyond the point to which you can endure, but will with the testing also make the way of escape that you may be able to bear it. May the Lord so fill your life in His own way with the people and the purposes of His choice, and the strength to fulfil your part, that aloneness never degenerates into painful loneliness for you.

If you have not been troubled personally with the oppressive monster of loneliness, will you do all in your power to ease the burden and brighten the pathway for some lonely soul? And let me remind you again of our Royal Saviour's words: 'Inasmuch as you have done it unto one of the least of these My brethren, you have done it unto Me' (Matt. 25:40).

Chapter 5

WORRY

If you stand near the exit of a London Tube station and watch people coming out you will see some emerging buoyantly, with confident step and keen, alert eyes. You will see some young couples walking out as if on air, with that 'You can't imagine how wonderful is the world we are living in!' look in their eyes. But the impression you will be almost certain to get, not only at King's Cross, is that the majority have a tired, worried look on their faces. You may blame travel by Tube. But you would be wide of the mark if you blame it all on the journey, however nerve-racking it is in the rush hour.

What makes you look worried? How often does your wife, or husband, or mother, have to say to you: 'Don't look so worried'? Looking worried is only the symptom. Those who look worried generally *are* worried. All sensible people are *concerned* about important things. But concern too often deteriorates into worry, and lawful anxiety becomes over-anxiety.

FACING THE PROBLEM

There must be very few people alive today, Christians as well as non-Christians, who are not attacked in some way or other by this giant of modern society – worry.

What is worry? No doubt some facetious reader will reply: 'Why worry to define it?' The dictionary defines worry as 'a disturbed state of mind, anxiety'. It goes on to define something that is 'a worry' as 'anything that causes anxiety or disturbs tranquillity.'

We hardly need to ask whether worry does any harm. Some people's hair has been turned white overnight through shock and very intense worry. But not all prematurely white-haired people are to be thought of as great worriers. We have all heard of worry driving people to an early grave. We talk of 'the worry of it' driving us 'up the wall' or 'round the bend'. We know how worry eats into our sleep, takes the joy out of life, robs us of our appetites, takes our minds off people we are supposed to be talking to and paints the future black and grim and forbidding.

What are the causes of worry? Naturally enough, these vary with the individual, and in the experience of each individual they vary with different phases of life. The schoolboy worries about his exams, or his spots, or being found out. The girl worries about her personal appearance, her clothes, her colour schemes, her chances. The young father worries about insurance policies, schooling, his own promotion, while his wife worries about making ends meet, keeping the place looking respectable and getting replacements earlier than they had budgeted for, because they never dreamed the rising generation would spring up so quickly! Or she may worry about keeping her husband's affection when she is over forty. One worries about her house and anybody disturbing the way she puts things. Another worries about her health, with cancer or thrombosis as the ogres bearing down upon her from the distant horizon. Others worry about retirement and failing health or failing memory.

Now these are all very natural and perfectly understandable worries. Some of them help us to take life seriously and challenge us to our maximum effort. The athlete who never gets 'needle' is not likely to run a mile under four minutes or stroke Cambridge to victory. The examination candidate who never 'gets the butterflies' is not likely to get a distinction. Knowing that others think you are capable of making the top grade, and fearing that you may not do it, lays you open to a nervous tension that may never afflict the person from whom nobody expects much anyway. It helps to key you up to the required pitch of concentration.

Temperament and disposition enter into this, as well as capacity. We must also make allowances for up-bringing. We cannot say that all worry is harmful or sinful.

But there are other causes of worry which go deeper than the things we have been thinking about so far. There is the worry that comes from unforgiven sin. A doctor said to me, not long ago: 'It would be a very good thing if far more people were worried more about their sins and less about their bodies, which they are going to leave behind, anyway, in a few years.'

FINDING THE ANSWER

Some years ago a woman went to a Harley Street specialist about her worries. His prescription at the end of the consultation was rather a shock to her: 'Read the Bible for half an hour each evening.' It was as effective as it was unexpected, and was well worth the fee! Reading the Bible is not the answer to every worry, but there is no doubt that if we read our Bibles more we should worry less. The more we read the Bible, the more impressed we become with God's faithfulness. The more we see He is faithful, the more natural it is to trust Him. The more we trust Him, the less we worry. The external problems don't always change. But we do. And often the greatest difficulty lies not so much in the awkward things themselves as in our attitude to them.

Reading the Bible regularly is good preventive medicine for the human mind and spirit. You can't be bounced into panic or get worried in the same way as others whose only Bible is the newspapers, if you hide God's Word in your heart every day.

I hide Thy Word, not knowing when
The testing time may be,
Or soon, or late, but sure that then
It will be true to me.

But reading the Bible can do more than preserve us from the tyranny of worry. It can point the way to cure when we have failed to use it as 'preventive medicine'. There are clear statements of fact in the Bible which are the specific remedy for certain major forms of worry. 'Hoping for the best' and 'keeping your fingers crossed' is not the answer.

WORRY ABOUT THE PAST

For many conscientious people, and even some who have been pretty unscrupulous in the past, the chief worry is a sense of failure. 'We have done those things which we ought not to have done, and we have left undone those things which we ought to have done.' Those jealous thoughts, that impure imagination, that mean, despicable thing, that duty you dodged, that kindness you wouldn't show, that forgiveness you wouldn't give, those words that ran off your tongue before you knew what a cutting edge they had – all these and many other things disturb the conscience. Let me warn you that your conscience cannot find peace about these things until you are forgiven. There is no real peace for unforgiven men and women. Be honest with yourself. Does your chief worry centre in the past? It doesn't have to be 'a skeleton in the cupboard'. A series of little things can have just as devastating an effect on us. Have you tried to forget it all and found you couldn't? It is hard to forget what is not forgiven. Is your present life marred by a sense of guilt, an awareness of failure, a sense of shame over it? Is your future over-clouded by shadows that hang over from your failure in the past, like damage left by a receding flood? Then I have good news for you. You may be forgiven and so find peace concerning your past. Peace follows forgiveness as surely as day follows dawn.

It was to make forgiveness possible for the man with sin on his conscience that God sent His Son into this world. 'Christ Jesus came into the world to save sinners' (I Tim. 1:15). 'Who His own self bare our sins in His own body on the tree' (I Pet. 2:24, cf. 3:18). 'If we confess our sins, He is faithful and just to forgive us our sins, and to cleanse us from all unrighteousness' (I John 1:8,9).

This does not mean that you have only to tell God you are sorry and He will forgive you. Sorry you must be – so sorry that you want to do all you can to put things right, so sorry that you never want to do such a thing again, but sorry, most of all, that your sin cost God so much. 'Christ died for our sins.' How awful sin must be in God's sight if such a sacrifice was needed to put it right! But the sacrifice has been made, and the blood of Christ can cleanse the conscience from every stain.

Do you realise your sinfulness and guilt before God? Will you turn from going your own way to the Christ who died for sinful men? Will you confess your sins? Do you believe Christ died for your sins? Will you thank Him from the bottom of your heart for bearing the punishment due to your sins? Will you ask Him for the strength to put right all you can, to apologise sincerely where you can, to put back what is not yours? Then you can be sure that the blood of Christ, God's Son, cleanses you from all sin. You will be forgiven for Christ's sake. And the worry about an unforgiven past will leave you, even if the memory stays (I John 1:7; 2:12; Eph. 4:32). God has promised, for His part, to remember your sins no more (Heb. 10:17;

Micah 7:18,19).

Mind you, it is not enough to tell God you are sorry if you know you have hurt somebody else by word or deed. You must tell them you are sorry, too, and do something about it, if fair compensation can be made (Matt. 5:23,24). I know there are many situations in which compensation is not possible. And if your sin was sin in thought (jealousy, lust, etc.), let it be confessed to God alone, who knows your thought-life through and through, as well as the rest of your complex personality. To confess such thoughts to somebody else may not only break fellowship and cause unnecessary embarrassment but even, in some cases, defile other minds.

Leaving the past with God, we can no longer worry about it in the same way, though we may still carry through life some pretty sad memories.

But there are many whose burning problem is

WORRY ABOUT THE PRESENT

The focal point of this worry may be a relationship with another person living under the same roof. It is most wearing to live day in and day out with people you don't get on with. 'Incompatibility of temperament' (where the other person's 'chips' don't fit into the chips on your own shoulder!) is a phrase that accounts for much domestic unhappiness. It may be interpreted as 'inability to give and take on a scale big enough to make for harmonious living'.

So many impatient youngsters rush into marriage merely on the basis of physical attraction and emotional infatuation, going by looks instead of liking, cosmetic finish instead of character. And all too many of them discover that their interests and temperaments just don't fit, and they can't hit it off properly when the first novelty of being together all the time has worn off.

There is a lot of truth in the old saying, 'Marry in haste, repent at leisure.' Somebody may ask: 'Can I get free without going against God?' The answer is: Yes, you can get free, but not from your partner! You can get free from what makes you so difficult to live with. And, by and by, your life-partner may come to the same Liberator for freedom. 'If the Son shall make you free, ye shall be free indeed' (John 8:36). Domestic triangles are not automatically resolved by the conversion to Christ of one of the conflicting parties, but the new patience, new love and real prayers of the new Christian cannot be in vain (I Pet. 3:1,2).

A sense of inadequacy, developing in some people into a thorough-going 'inferiority complex', may be your particular worry. There is some problem too much for you in your own life, or in your home, friendship or work. If you have come to Christ already, for cleansing from your past sins, God has the answer. But you cannot expect His strength for the present or His guidance for the future if your past has not been dealt with. What is God's answer? Paul, the great apostle, found it, and so can we. He says, 'For this thing (a thorn in the flesh) I besought the Lord thrice, that it might depart from me. And He said unto me, My grace is sufficient for you: for My strength is made perfect in weakness. Most gladly therefore will I rather glory in my infirmities, that the power of Christ may rest upon me...for when I am weak, then am I strong' (II Cor. 12:7-10). 'I can do all things (I can face all circumstances, I am ready for anything) through Christ who strengthens me' (Phil. 4:13). The more weakness, sense of inadequacy, I bring Him, the greater the opportunity for Him to display His saving strength.

How often I have had to tell Him: 'Lord, I can't cope.' But I don't stop there, for what I cannot do, He can with the greatest of ease. So my prayer is: 'Lord, I cannot cope, but Thou canst. Please *take my weakness* in this situation, and *make Your strength perfect in it*. Do *for* me that which I cannot do. Do *through* me that which I cannot do. Do *with* me what You will. Do all that is needed *in spite of* me, where I am in Your way, for Christ's sake. Amen.' And He does.

Nothing is a nuisance to Him, however small it may be. Nothing is so big that it presents a problem to Him. 'Never forget the nearness of your Lord. Don't worry over anything whatever; tell God every detail of your needs in earnest and thankful prayer, and the peace of God, which transcends human understanding, will keep constant guard over your hearts and minds as they rest in Christ Jesus...fix your minds on the things which are holy and right and pure and beautiful and good...and you will find that the God of peace will be with you' (Phil. 4:5-9 J.B. Phillips).

If there are those who cannot enjoy the present because they are so pressed down with the mess they have made of the past, there are many more whose enjoyment of the present is completely ruined by

WORRY ABOUT THE FUTURE

Have you an over-active imagination which projects you into a terrifying future? The Scripture gives this assurance: 'You will keep him in perfect peace, whose mind is stayed on You' (Isa. 26:3).

Are you afraid you will not be able to hold out under pressure of certain temptations or testings? 'No temptation has (or can) come your way that is too hard for flesh and blood to bear. But God can be trusted not to allow you to suffer any temptation (or testing) beyond your powers of endurance. He will see to it that every temptation has a way out, so that it will never be impossible for you to bear it' (I Cor. 10:13 J.B. Phillips).

Are you afraid you may be left on the shelf? 'No good thing will He withhold from those who walk uprightly' (Ps. 84:11). If married life is a good thing for you in His eyes He will lead you to the partner of His choice in His own time. But it is better to go through life alone in happy fellowship with the Saviour than to be tied up to an undedicated partner who tries to come between you and your Lord.

Is your worry that you may not be able to retain your life-partner's affections as middle-age creeps on relentlessly? Bring your capacity to love to Him each day and you will lose your fears as He fills you afresh with His presence and His love. (See John 4:14; 7:37-39; Gal. 5:22-23; I Cor. 13:1-8).

Are you afraid you may miss your life-purpose? Let the Lord Jesus have every scrap of your being every day, and you can count on Him to unfold His blue-print for you (Rom. 12:1,2).

Is your worry the fear of some crippling illness or premature death? Take reasonable precautions, and leave body, soul and spirit in His hands. It is always safe to trust the Lord Jesus with absolutely everything. (See Ps. 37:1-9; Rom. 12:1,2; I Thess. 5:23-24).

Are you worried about the possibilities of nuclear war and the end of civilisation? 'Don't worry, it may never happen' is hardly the answer! What is the answer? Plan as though you were going to live a full life to a ripe old age, but live as though your Lord is coming tonight. Men's hearts are failing them for fear as they realise what is threatening the world. But *Jesus is coming again*.

There is no need to despair. Christ is the hope of the believer as well as the light of the world. Lift up your heads, for your redemption is drawing near. (See Luke 21:24-28).

Finally, are you afraid of being lost, rejected at heaven's gate? If your trust has been placed in the Lord

Jesus He will *never* let go of you. You cannot be snatched by an enemy or circumstance out of His strong grip. 'They shall never perish' (John 10:28), but are 'kept by the power of God' (I Pet. 1:5).

So, however seriously you may take life, don't worry any more, but *trust* in the Lord with all your heart (Prov. 3:5,6). Take firm hold of some of His promises, and keep them constantly before your mind. 'Casting all your care upon Him, for He cares for you' (I Pet. 5:7). J.B. Phillips translates it: 'You can rest the weight of all your anxieties upon Him, for you are always in His care.' He cannot let you down. For He is God and must keep His word.

'Now unto Him that is able to keep you from falling, and to present you faultless before the presence of His glory with exceeding joy, to the only wise God our Saviour, be glory and majesty, dominion and power, both now and ever. Amen' (Jude 24,25).

Chapter 6

DEATH

INTRODUCTION

My heart goes out to all who have been bereaved. Even if you have been watching a loved one sinking farther week by week, day by day, it still comes as something of a shock when the actual parting comes. May God bring to any reader who has been bereaved recently the comfort He has for you, whether through the following lines or in spite of them.

The angel of death comes to different people at very different times of life. Sometimes death brings welcome relief to the watchers as well as to the person dying, because life has become such an awful burden – 'labour and sorrow', as the Psalmist calls it. And sometimes we have no explanation of the timing. Why should such a person die so young? All we can do is trust the higher wisdom of the One who sends His angel and believe that 'as for God His way is perfect'. His way includes His timing.

Some babies are unwanted. They were not planned. They tie down the parents. They are an embarrassment to them economically. But this baby was not one of these. It was longed for, prayed for, eagerly awaited. And when it came, it was still-born. The face of the world was grey for the parents that day. Did God not care? Of course He did. He loved them so much that He sent His Son to die for them. And now He had called their own wee son before he could respond to their eager love. The Lord gave. The Lord had taken away. Blessed be the name of the Lord. They would not impeach His character. He knew what He was doing even if they didn't. And they crept close under His overshadowing hand. They believed God. And today they are joyfully watching the boy God gave them a year later, as he grows up, the picture of health – a bonny, bouncing boy, with a wee brother already in heaven.

Another child was less than a year old when he was taken from the loving arms of his parents. Could they turn round on God and curse Him? No, they couldn't do that. The words that brought the most comfort to them in their grief were, 'I shall go to him, but he shall not return to me' (II Sam. 12:15-23). Those little fingers had twined themselves round the hearts of those loving parents. But other fingers had been nailed to a cross for that darling boy and for themselves, and they were content to leave their treasure in the hands of Him who says, 'I am...the Living one; and I was dead, and behold, I am alive for evermore, and I have the keys of death...' (Rev. 1:18 R.V.).

Another couple had been married for a number of years, and it seemed that the child they longed to crown their love with was never going to come. So they adopted – a very sensible thing to do. Ten happy years went by. One day, their chosen treasure went to play near the canal with his friends. He was drowned. Grief-stricken, the parents wondered why. Father tried to drown his sorrow in wine. Mother could not control her tears. She just went on and on weeping. One day she heard of Jesus in a new way. He was the Son who was taken from His mother in the full beauty of His manhood. She saw, too, that He had died for her, giving Himself a ransom that she might be set free from her sorrow. She believed that it was He, and not an 'inexorably cruel fate' that had called her boy to His side. She yielded her broken heart to the Saviour and asked Him to take her and fulfil through her some of the lovely things He would have done through her dear boy if He had spared him to his manhood. Her grief was no longer inconsolable. God wiped away her tears. She saw that He could look after her boy far better in His heavenly home than she could in her earthly home.

Three teenage friends went out for a walk on Southampton Common on a lovely August day. The sky clouded over and a great storm burst suddenly upon them. They sought shelter under a large tree. Lightning flashed. Three promising young lives lay dead on the ground. Just a few weeks before, they had heard the call of Christ and had responded. They were now living in the full joy of clear-cut Christian faith. When the call came, so suddenly, so unexpectedly, they were ready. And on one of the gravestones may be read the words: 'Jesus called a child unto Him.'

Peter was twenty-four, working hard at a teacher training college. He had been a Christian for almost two years and was witnessing effectively to his fellow-students by the conversations he steered round naturally to Christian things, by his cheerful fine-quality life, by his high moral standards and his hard work. He had seen his mother turn to the Lord soon after his own conversion. But Peter was a diabetic, and one night when his sugar balance got wrong the Lord called him in his sleep.

'Have you seen a difference in your son during these past two years?' the grief-stricken father was asked.

'Yes, a tremendous difference,' he replied.

'Do you put it down to his new-found faith?'

'Yes, I do,' answered the father.

'Has this made you want to share his faith and carry on his good work where he has had to leave off?'

Peter's father made it quite clear in answer to this question that there was nothing he wanted more. There and then, in a hotel bedroom not far from the college, he knelt beside his weeping wife and a Christian friend and solemnly committed himself to the Lord Jesus for

His forgiveness, cleansing, newness of life and life-plan. And the plan is being fulfilled, with Peter's younger brother part of the team now. Truly, 'God moves in a mysterious way His wonders to perform.' What a wonderful reunion there is going to be for this family one day! They trust, but they can also trace. Enough of the pattern is visible for them to be able to see what good sense it all makes. Once again we must say, 'As for God, His way is perfect.'

THE LAST ENEMY – DEATH

No one can go through bereavement or even attend a funeral without wondering, 'Where are the dead?' This question may be brushed aside through fear, for fear of death is probably more widespread than most of us realise. Or the question may be dismissed by saying to oneself, whether wistfully or half-defiantly or self-defensively, 'Nobody knows. In any case it is not for me to ask such profound questions.'

'Theology is not my line,' some say, though they may wish they had time to read up some of the literature on this great subject. Others consider that any thought given to death is sheer escapism. Many of our quite seriously minded contemporaries think that people who waste precious time thinking about 'pie in the sky when they die' need to be brought down to earth with a bump. Those who were behind the popular surge of Humanism, which was affecting many sincere young people, included among their leading doctrines a flat denial of any life after this. This life is all, and is enough, they think.

But the subject of death can hardly be called irrelevant or escapist to any man, whether humanist, agnostic or Christian. Death is inescapable. Death comes to all of us. Death is perhaps the only thing we can be sure of in this uncertain life! Graduation is not a certainty for the undergraduate. Marriage is not a certainty for the engaged couple. But, apart from the generation alive at the second coming of Christ, death is an absolute certainty. And death is so final as far as this life is concerned that no thinking man should reason that death is irrelevant or unimportant. He who plans his life without allowing for death is a fool. We never know when death may come. It is not only old men and women, or soldiers and sailors in action and people involved in air crashes who die. While it is true that most people in the West die in old age, there are enough exceptions to this rule for us to need to be ready to face death long before we reach old age.

WHAT IS THERE AFTER DEATH?

'If a man die, shall he live again?' asked Job, some three thousand years ago or more. This is a question people are still asking and will go on asking so long as death exists. And there are several popular answers to this question.

The Agnostic answers: Nobody who is still alive knows. The dead may know. But dead men tell no tales, and no one has ever come back to tell us. The only life you can be sure of is this life. Let us make the most of it.

The Atheist pushes the answer still further. He assures us that there is absolutely nothing after death. You can make this life a heaven or a hell. There is none other. Death is annihilation. Death ends everything.

'When I die,' says Bertrand Russell in *Why I am not a Christian*, 'I shall rot, and nothing of my ego will survive...I am not afraid.' Many who think and feel like this choose cremation in preference to ordinary burial in case they are wrong! As if that makes it more difficult for the great Creator to summon them to the bar of His judgement!

The Buddhist has a different answer. And many who would not dream of calling themselves Buddhists would readily give the same answer. After death comes reincarnation. And this must not be limited to a second chance, for a man would need many chances until, through a process of gradual betterment, he reaches at last that extinction of personality which the Buddhist calls nirvana. The consequence of this theory for practical living is that life is not all that important. There are other lives to come. It doesn't matter too much if we make a mess of things now. We can always come back again as someone or something else and have another go. There will be plenty of opportunities to improve! Time is on our side. Life after death need hold no terrors for us.

The Universalist joins hands with the Mormon in assuring us that we are all going to a happy place. There is a heaven for everybody. The Mormon would urge us to be baptised as Mormons and have our marriage sealed in one of their Temples if we are going to be candidates for the highest grades of heaven (godhood), but even those who fall by the Mormon wayside will get in somewhere comfortable in the end. There is no hell according to their teaching. God is far too good to allow anyone to exist in such a miserable place.

The Spiritualists have another answer. There is no hell. But there is a spirit-world to which all men go the moment they die. Jesus Christ is not what most Christians think He is. He is an advanced spirit on one of the higher planes of existence in the Great Beyond. The spirits of the departed are still desperately interested in their loved ones on earth. They want to assure us of their well-being so that we may not worry about them. They often have important guidance for us when we come to a crossroads on the journey through life. So it is wise, they say, for us to get in touch with a local medium who may be able to get this information through to us. Small beginnings with a planchette in a nurses' common-room or a fellow-student's bedroom (women's colleges suffer more from this than men's!) can lead to dangerous voyages of discovery in the spirit-world.

Roman Catholics, Anglo-Catholics and some Orthodox Churchmen have more or less one answer between them. Purgatory is the next stage for most of us. Limbo is the place for unbaptised infants and for others not worthy of punishment in hell, such as the mentally incompetent who die 'without grievous personal guilt' (*Catholic Encyclopaedia*, IX, p.256). This explains the anxiety of Roman Catholic nurses to baptise infants whose lives seem to be in danger. Immediate entrance to heaven is restricted to a small, very select company — saints who by their great holiness and the wisely directed merits of others have won this glorious privilege. Masses said for the departed can speed up progress through purgatory. Adults who were never baptised, and all who have committed unabsolved mortal sin after baptism, go to hell immediately they die.

HOW CAN WE KNOW THE TRUTH?

How are we to know which of these voices competing for our attention is right? Some would say we cannot be sure; you just have to hope that the ideas that appeal to you most are the right ideas. But the Christian who is familiar with the teaching of Holy Scripture says you *can* be sure. God has given us in the Bible all we need to know about life after death. Let us consider what the Bible says in the face of these answers.

To the Agnostic the Bible says: God has appointed a day in which He will judge the world in righteousness by that Man whom He has ordained, and He has given assurance of this in that He raised Him from the dead. (See Acts 17:31.) Someone *has* come back from death. And He will one day be the Judge – or Saviour – of every man. None can escape this judgement. He is the Saviour of all those who trust Him. Their works will come under His scrutiny, though their eternal salvation is not at stake. (See John 5:24; I Cor. 3:10-15.)

To the Atheist the Bible says: Once it is appointed to man to die, but after this the judgement (Heb. 9:27). There is a resurrection both of the just and of the unjust (Acts 24:15). The hour is coming, in which all that are in the graves shall hear His (Christ's) voice, and shall come forth, those who have done good to the resurrection of life, and those who have done evil to the resurrection of damnation (John 5:28,29).

To the Universalist, whether Mormon or not, the Bible says there is a hell to be shunned as well as a heaven to be sought. Christ will say to some: 'Depart from Me, you cursed, into everlasting fire, prepared for the devil and his angels.' To His own He will say: 'Come, you blessed by My Father, inherit the kingdom prepared for you from the foundation of the world' (Matt. 25:41,34).

To the Spiritualist the Bible has some very straight things to say. Necromancy (seeking to contact the dead, as in Spiritualism) is an abomination to the Lord. The Canaanites were driven out of the land in Old Testament times because of these things (Deut. 18:10-14). They gave to spirits the place that belongs to God. Saul's crowning sin was going to a medium instead of seeking God (I Sam. 28). The New Testament teaches that spirits are to be tested, and not trusted just because they are obviously supernatural. Only a spirit confessing that Jesus is truly the Son of God is a spirit that comes from God (I John 4:1-4).

To a Buddhist and all those who believe in reincarnation, the Bible gives the same answer as to those who think there is no judgement to be faced hereafter. But to them the emphasis needs to be placed on the first part of Hebrews 9:27: 'It is appointed unto men once to die, but after this the judgement.' Reincarnation cannot be reconciled with that unambiguous 'once'. For reincarnation would involve as many experiences of passing through death as there are incarnations. And the Scripture emphasises the once-for-all-ness of this experience of death by the rest of the sentence quoted above: As it is appointed unto men once to die...so Christ was once offered for sin. He who suffered under Pontius Pilate, was crucified and buried once. It is never to happen to Him again. Nor will physical death come to any man twice.

To Roman Catholics and Anglo-Catholics the Bible speaks of the believer departing immediately at death to be with Christ, and describes this as far better than life on earth. The atoning death of Christ is totally sufficient to purge away all our sins. To suggest that more is needed is to cast reflection on the provision God has made. When a sinner comes to Christ in true repentance he is ready to go to heaven immediately, without a moment in purgatory. His life may need considerable transforming on earth, but it is not this that fits him for heaven. Christ's justifying work fits us for heaven. Christ's sanctifying work fits us for a life on earth that glorifies Him. The Bible knows nothing of any purgatory. The only verse quoted by Catholics in support of purgatory is I Corinthians 3:15, which is in a context that deals with a Christian's service and not with his salvation.

The Bible answers many other questions about life after death, and we shall now look at some of the most important of these.

THE CERTAINTY OF LIFE AFTER DEATH

This certainty comes out quite clearly in the Old Testament. The *patriarchs* spoke of joining their fathers in sleep at death. Job was even more explicit. He declared with passionate feeling, 'I know that my Redeemer lives, and that He shall stand at the latter day upon the earth; and after my body is destroyed, with my own personality shall I see God. I shall see Him for myself'. (See Job 19:25-27.)

Isaiah spoke with ringing conviction of a great resurrection day that is surely coming, when God 'will swallow up death in victory; and the Lord God will wipe away tears from off all faces'. On this day 'your dead men shall live, together with my dead body shall they arise' (Isa. 25:8; 26:19).

Solomon knew there was a fundamental difference between an animal and a human being. At death the life of an animal comes to an end. It was not made in the image of God. But when a human dies, the body returns to its constituent elements, but the spirit returns to God who gave it (Eccl. 12:7; 3:21).

The expectations of believers in the living God in Old Testament days are summed up magnificently by the writer to the Hebrews, when he says, 'they desire a better country, that is, an heavenly' (Heb.11:16).

But it is in the New Testament that we find the fullest answer concerning this question of life after death. Here we find mankind divided into two groups, the saved and the lost, with two destinies, heaven and hell. There are many illustrations of this division, e.g. the parables of the wheat and the tares, the good and bad fish, the sheep and the goats (Matt. 13 and 25). And there are explicit statements about this division, as we have seen — e.g. in Jesus Christ's declaration that in the day of Judgement 'all that are in the graves... shall come forth; those who have done good, unto the

resurrection of life; and those who have done evil, unto
the resurrection of damnation' (John 5:28,29). It is
more certain than tomorrow's dawn that there is a
resurrection both of the just and of the unjust (Acts
24:15).

WHERE ARE THE BELIEVING DEAD?

Having looked at some of the popular, contemporary
ideas about life after death, and considered what the
Bible says about resurrection in general, let us take
a closer look at what the Bible teaches about the
believing dead. It is not God's will that we should stay
completely in the dark about this subject. This is one
reason why God's servant says in I Thessalonians 4:13,
'I would not have you to be ignorant, brethren,
concerning those who are asleep'.

Death comes to all

Death is no respecter of persons. Until Christ comes
again, death comes to Christians and non-Christians
alike, whether through old age, disease, accident or
war. The Bible speaks of 'death' in more than one
sense: (a) Physical death, which is the separation of the
spirit from the body. (b) Spiritual death, which means
being out of touch with God, 'dead in trespasses and
sins' (Eph. 2:1-3). (c) The second death, which is the
final separation of the unbeliever from God (Rev.
21:8).

Christians need not fear death

Those who trust in Christ are already spiritually alive
and in touch with God. The second death cannot touch
them. Physical death is all they have to face. We may
shrink from the process of dying, because the way is

unfamiliar and the circumstances may be painful. But the Son of God took our humanity that through His death He might take away our fear of death. Just before he died for his faith, Bishop Nicholas Ridley wrote: 'Why should we Christians fear death? Can death deprive us of Christ, who is all our comfort, our joy, and our life? No indeed, death shall deliver us from this mortal body, which burdens and bears down upon the spirit so that it cannot so well perceive heavenly things.'

One of the favourite poems of John Stam, who with his wife Betty was martyred by Communist bandits in China in 1934, was written by another missionary to China, the Rev. E.H. Hamilton, when a fellow-worker of his, the Rev. J.W. Vinson, was put to death for his faith and work.

Afraid? Of what?
To feel the spirit's glad release,
To pass from pain to perfect peace,
The strife and strain of life to cease –
Afraid – of that?

Afraid? Of what?
Afraid to see the Saviour's face,
To hear His welcome and to trace
The glory gleam from wounds of grace?
Afraid – of that?

Afraid? Of what?
A flash, a crash, a pierced heart;
Darkness, light – O Heaven's art,
A wound of His the counterpart,
Afraid – of that?

Afraid? Of what?
To enter into heaven's rest,
And still to serve the Master blest,
From service good to service best –
Afraid –   of that?

A woman who was riddled with cancer came from her village somewhere near 'the roof of the world' to the missionary doctor in a distant town.

'Am I going to get better, doctor?' she asked.

'I am afraid you are not likely to,' replied the doctor.

'Then let me stay here and learn of your faith. I am so afraid of dying. My brother will build me a hut. I won't be in your way. Let me die here.'

She drank in the Christian message, came to the Lord Jesus and found in Him the peace which the world can neither give nor take away. The disease increased its grip on her body, but her face grew radiant.

Presently her new Master made His will quite clear to her.

'I must go back to my village. I haven't got long to tell them what I have found.'

So back she went and told all her friends and neighbours what the Lord Jesus had done for her. A few days later she gathered a group of women together for the missionary doctor to speak to.

After the message was delivered she said, 'I would like to die now. I am so tired.'

The next time the missionary doctor came that way the villagers told her, 'It was wonderful how she died! She wasn't afraid. We are all so afraid of dying.'

Death for the Christian is going home

The body may be looked on as a cottage in which our

earthly days are lived. In the moment of death, before the body can be laid to rest until the resurrection day, the inhabitant of the cottage moves out, or 'flits' as the Scots say so expressively.

The lights are all out in the mansion of clay,
The curtains are drawn for the dweller's away;
She silently slipped o'er the threshold by night
To make her abode in the city of light.

For the Christian, death is the doorway to heaven. When he dies he is absent from the body and at home with the Lord. There is no waiting in any purgatorial corridors of varying lengths. Never will those of us who are Christians be more grateful for the atoning death of the Lord Jesus Christ than when we find ourselves instantly welcomed into His presence, brought safely home through His sacrifice. The last judgement has no terrors for those whose trust is in the Redeemer. We have this assurance on the highest authority. The Saviour said, 'In very truth, anyone who gives heed to what I say and puts his trust in Him who sent Me, has hold of (possesses) eternal life (notice the present tense), and does not come up for judgement, but has already passed from death to life' (John 5:24 N.E.B.). There is no condemnation for the man or woman who is united to Christ by personal faith. Paul spoke of his longing to depart to be with Christ, which is far better than the best experience on earth. When Stephen was dying he saw heaven opened, and Jesus standing at the right hand of God, the place of power and final authority. Jesus was standing to welcome His servant into the heavenly home! 'Lord Jesus, receive my spirit,' were Stephen's last words (Acts 7:55-60). Wonderful last words! We could not say better.

Some Christians hear the songs of angels just before God calls them home. Some see the faces of loved ones waiting to greet them. A veteran missionary to Spain was whispering something as he lay dying. A Christian Spanish girl knelt beside him and caught the words, 'The doors are opened. I see Jesus. Hallelujah!'

People ask what heaven is really like. The Bible does not tell us all there is to know about heaven. But there are plenty of clues. When Paul was caught up into Paradise, the third heaven, perhaps after his stoning at Lystra, he heard the most wonderful things which the Holy Spirit would not allow him to record. It may be that God could see that if we knew too much about heaven while on earth, we would neglect our earthly duties! But He has shown enough for us to know that heaven is a wonderful place.

Heaven is a place of fellowship

To us on earth the dead are asleep, unconscious. To God in heaven they are wide awake, in the presence of Christ their Saviour. They were never more alive than they are now! In His presence they now have the full, unbroken communion that they often longed for, but never completely achieved on earth because of the limitations of time and sense.

Do you sometimes wonder whether we shall recognise one another in heaven? Of course we will — as surely as the disciples recognised the risen Lord. How could the Thessalonian Christians be Paul's 'joy' in Christ's presence unless he recognised them? We shall be like Him, recognisably. Yet we shall be ourselves, equally recognisably. Human relationships will not be on the same basis as on earth. There is no marriage in heaven, for example, because there is no death and no need for a new generation to replace the old. But fellowship between Christians will be more wonderful than anything they have experienced on earth. The bond of love in heaven is stronger than the strongest bonds on earth.

Heaven is a place of rest

During our life on earth, we Christians may often be puzzled and perplexed. We may go through trouble and pain, failure and sorrow, mental pressure, and even persecution. But the moment we die, rest comes. And nothing can disturb that rest. Frustration, disappointments, heartaches, disease, fears and sorrows – all are gone and gone for ever.

All the mysteries of life which have made us ask, 'Why has God allowed this to happen?' are fully explained then by a loving Heavenly Father. In our life-time we have to trust Him where we cannot trace His ways. But then we will see things from God's point of view and will be able to get everything in true perspective, not just from a limited, human viewpoint. Then we will know even as also we are known. Perfection has come at last; perfect love, perfect knowledge, perfect rest.

Heaven is a place of joy

In His presence is fullness of joy. No one is ever sad in heaven. None of the things that cause unhappiness on earth can enter heaven. There is no unkindness, no cruelty, no selfishness, no loneliness. 'And God shall wipe away all tears from their eyes; and there shall be no more death, neither sorrow, nor crying, neither shall there be any more pain' (Rev. 21:4).

Many a child in a Christian home asks, 'Will I be able to have my doll (or Teddy or bicycle or electric train or ice-cream) in heaven?' The accompanying look or the tone of voice implies that heaven has little or no attraction if the answer is No! Most children are perfectly satisfied with an answer something like this:

'If you still want it when you get to heaven, you will find it there. The Lord Jesus has everything to make boys and girls happy.' As children get older they can understand more readily that the Lord will satisfy them completely without the material things that make a child's 'heaven'.

Nobody, adult or child, should imagine heaven will be dull, for at His 'right hand there are pleasures for evermore' (Ps. 16:11). We shall see Him as He is. And He is altogether lovely.

Heaven is a place of service

'His servants shall serve Him' (Rev. 22:3). And their motives will be as pure as their love. Service without rest could be exhausting and uninspiring. Rest without service could be monotonous. But heaven contains both, in perfect balance, in the wisdom of God. It may well be that the greatest service still lies in the future for the believers who have died. They are waiting for their resurrection bodies, which they will receive when Christ returns in power and great glory to this world in which He was crucified. I Thessalonians 4:13-18 and I Corinthians 15:35-54 give us a glimpse of this wonderful prospect. The believing dead are waiting for the full reward of their labours (Matt. 25: 14-23). They already possess eternal life as the free gift which God gives to all who believe in His Son (Rom. 6:23). But a crown of life is yet to be received by those who stood up to severe tests for His sake (Jas. 1:12). God looks on them as being righteous already, clothed in the righteousness of Christ (Rom 5:1-11). But a crown of righteousness will be given, when Christ comes, to all who love His appearing (II Tim. 4:8).

What a relief to be able to leave our believing dead in His strong hands. They do not need our prayers. Heaven needs no prompting as to how to care for its

own! What a joy for Christians to look forward to being
with Christ in heaven at the end of their earthly
pilgrimage.

You would I serve with all the strength You're giving,
  You would I love and honour and obey,
Until You call to live where You're now living,
  Where earth's dark shadows end in perfect day.

To see You as You are in all Your beauty,
  To gaze upon Your face and hear Your voice,
Then worship at Your feet will not be duty,
  But that at which my heart will most rejoice!

To serve You in the land where there's no parting,
  Unhindered by the drag of mortal frame,
And feel the Holy Spirit's fullest prompting
  Will make me give all glory to Your name!

WHAT HAPPENS TO UNBELIEVERS?

What of those who die unbelieving? What if I die
without Christ? And the longer I live without Christ,
the more likely I am to die without Christ. Is there
really a hell as well as a heaven? Surely, thinking
people don't believe in a hell these days? I have heard
this said many times. And to be perfectly frank I must
admit that none of us likes the idea of hell. Speaking
very reverently, I don't think God likes the idea of hell.
Judgement has been called His 'strange act'. It is mercy
He delights in, not judgement (Micah 7:18-20). But,
sad to say, there are those who refuse His mercy.
  Is hell not real because the very idea is one from
which every sensitive person shrinks? Humanists and
atheistic materialists say of course it is not real. In their
view there is no life at all after death. And there are
religious people, some quite prominent in the religious

world, who agree with the materialists about hell, even if they believe there is a better sphere beyond this life for the good and for those who believe in God.

What men say

Religious leaders in Christendom give some very different answers to questions about hell. Generally speaking, the answers differ according to the attitude to Scripture taken by the person questioned.

Some say:

'There is no such place and no teaching about it from our Lord's lips. Anything about hell in the Gospel record was imported from Judaism. The Jewish reporters could not get over their Jewish prejudices and put into the Saviour's lips hard things He would never have said!' But once you accept this, where do you draw the line? How can we be sure of anything He said? Were the writers deliberately dishonest? People do not face persecution and martyrdom for what they know to be untrue! And what about the Holy Spirit's inspiration, guiding the writers of Scripture into all truth?

Some say:

'The whole idea of hell is nothing more than a psychological lever, a kind of religious bluff, on the same level as a threat issued by an immature or a rather foolish parent to stop a child doing something wrong.' But this approach is not worthy of the God of truth. He neither encourages us in vain nor warns us in vain.

Others say:

'There is no such place as hell after this life. The only hell there is, is the hell you make for yourself here on earth, or some particularly unpleasant time when others try "to give you hell".' This idea is completely at variance with the teaching of the Bible.

Others say:

'There is such a place as hell, but no one goes to it for ever. Either you come back into God's presence after a period of banishment — for punishment, on the one hand, and purging, on the other — or else you are exterminated, wiped out of existence in any shape or form, having suffered consciously something of what was due to you for the violation of God's laws and your own conscience.'

What the Bible says

Christians who take the Bible as their authority in all matters of faith and conduct must accept the teaching of Scripture about hell. These Christians are probably a minority among the religious voices heard in our land today, although their convictions have been held by faithful believers in every generation since the times of the apostles. I believe with all my heart that their proposition is the true one, though I shrink from the implications of what I believe about hell as readily as anyone who is sensitive to the thought of people suffering. Nevertheless, I believe it to be the only one that does justice to all the facts we find in the Holy Scriptures. I accept it because what my Lord says on any subject has final authority for me, no matter how unpalatable it may seem to be on the surface or how unpopular it may be with our contemporaries.

As surely as there is a heaven to look forward to, there is a hell to be shunned. There is such a place, after death, for those who reject Christ, and it is to be avoided at all costs, because once you have entered it there is no escape from it and no joy in it. 'There is no hell with a little heaven in it, any more than there is a heaven with a little hell in it' (George Macdonald).

The reality of hell

While the Lord delights to be known by His mercy and forgiveness, He is also known by the judgement He executes. No matter how much the wicked may get away with in this life, a day of reckoning is coming. In fact, were it not for the coming judgement, God might seem either unjust or powerless to exercise His justice in a world which is in such a mess. But cruel and evil men who die unrepentant will depart into hell, and with them will go all who turn their backs on God, however outwardly respectable they may have been.

It has been said that the road to hell is paved with good intentions; without God's gracious help, man's best intentions cannot get him anywhere; and many who know they should be living a different life keep putting off the day of repentance and faith. This road can also be perfumed as well as paved – perfumed with potent scent. The Bible warns against the kind of woman who can lead a man to his moral death, the woman whose house is the way to hell (Prov. 5 and 7; 9:13-18).

We cannot dismiss this with an impatient reference to Old Testament ideas. Our Lord speaks most clearly about the dangers of hell. 'It is better to lose...than to be cast into hell fire' (See Matt. 5:29,30.). 'Fear not them which kill the body, but are not able to kill the soul: but rather fear Him which is able to destroy both soul and body in hell' (Matt. 10:28). There is something worse than torture. There is something worse than death. There is hell. And hell is real.

The nature of hell

The believer goes to Paradise, a place of beauty, peace and joy. The Christ-rejecter goes to Hades,* a place of shadows, unhappiness and sorrow. Hades might be described as the ante-room to hell, the place where Christ-rejecters wait until the day of judgement, when the final sentence will be pronounced and their final banishment effected. From our Lord's words in Luke 16:23-28 we learn that this is a place of conscious perception, of conscious pain and anguish of mind and conscience. The conscience that was stifled on earth may have a deadly grip in Hades, but too late. The memory that could so quickly forget on earth the harm inflicted on others, or the help that was never given, will be unable to forget in Hades. 'Son, remember...' Hades is a place of personal retribution. This man, who never raised a finger to help Lazarus in his awful need at his very gate, is now suffering himself. It was Dante's *Inferno* and not the Bible that introduced demons as the agents of this torment.

Hades is a place of unfulfilled wishes and un-answered requests (v.27). It is a place of punishment, not just correction, and it is significant that the word translated by 'punishment' in Matthew 25:46 *(kolasis)* is used in modern Greek for hell. It is equally significant that the Greek word for 'everlasting' in this verse is the same as that for 'eternal'. The one is as far-reaching in its scope as the other. And in Mark 9 our Lord's solemn words about hell being a place where the consciousness of loss and pain goes on for ever are repeated three times (vs. 44-48).

Because of our nature and our behaviour, our law-breaking and our unbelief, we all deserve to go to hell. Yet hell was not prepared for men at all, but for the devil and his angels (Matt. 25:41). Where is hell? At the end of a Christless life. Who goes to hell? The devil and his angels, and, despite God's loving arms outstretched towards them, all those who have pushed God out of their lives. Blinded by the devil, they have become his tools and will finally follow their master to his fate.

The way of escape from going to hell

At tremendous cost God has opened the way of escape for sinful men. 'How can you escape the damnation of hell?' asked our Lord concerning the religious leaders of His day who rejected His claims (Matt. 23:33). How shall we escape if we neglect the great salvation He has provided asks the writer to the Hebrews? (See Heb. 2:1-3.) The way to escape hell and the way to enter heaven are one and the same. Jesus is the only Deliverer from the wrath to come. He knew what hell would mean, and He endured the infinite mental and spiritual suffering of Calvary to save from its awfulness all who will come to Him in repentance and faith. If we go to hell it is not God who is to blame.

There's a way back to God from the dark paths of sin,
There's a door that is open and you may go in,
At Calvary's cross is where you begin,
When you come as a sinner to Jesus.

God grant that no one who reads this book may go to that sad and lonely place called hell.

A final word to those of you who are mourning the passing of some member of your family or some friend. Sometimes when we are in church the things of God can seem very remote and the voice of God nothing more than a faint whisper. But at a time of bereavement the voice of God may come to us much more clearly. We may have a vague sense that a door has opened into eternity and 'Where will you spend eternity?' becomes a relevant question.

While these things are fresh in your mind, will you not come personally to the Lord Jesus? He alone can bring you to His Father. He says so. 'I am the way, the truth, and the life: no man cometh to the Father, but by Me' (John 14:6). There may never be a better time for you to come to Him than now.

Do you remember singing as a child:

He died that we might be forgiven,
He died to make us good,
That we might go at last to heaven,
Saved by His precious blood.

Will you come, as someone who is a sinner in the sight of God, needing forgiveness and cleansing, to Him who died that sinners might live? Will you ask Him to forgive you and cleanse you and to take your life and make you all He wants you to be in this world, until He calls you into eternity, ready to meet Him? His promise holds good, 'Him who comes to Me (her who comes to Me) I will in no wise cast out' (John 6:37).

Come to Him today. Tomorrow may be too late, and there is so much at stake — eternity, the glory of God, and your eternal joy and peace. 'Where will you spend eternity?'

*See Luke 16:23 (R.S.V.).

Chapter 7
DEPRESSION

This much longer chapter would never have been written but for the insistence of a Christian psychiatrist, later a consultant but now with Christ having died in his forties in Manchester. Other friends impressed upon me the need of something like this to put into the hands both of those suffering from depression and of those seeking to help the sufferers. Another Christian psychiatrist, high up in the profession brought his firm faith and great experience to bear upon this material, correcting and adding, deleting and remoulding. So that this chapter is every bit as much their work as mine. Perhaps I should say that the good things come from the Bible and these two specialists, and any blemishes in thought or presentation are mine.

Social workers, doctors, ministers and others are constantly meeting people who are suffering from depression in some form or another. This may not be your problem, but this chapter may give you some ideas with which you may be able to help others who are battling with depression.

A very few people suffer from depression through much of the day for most of their adult life. Some have fairly regular bouts when depression, like an internal 'smog', spreads a blanket of gloom and despair over everything. Some make great efforts to conceal their depression, and do this fairly successfully at times, depending on who they are with and where they are. But most really depressed people have a depressing effect on others when they are 'plumbing the depths'.

We need to distinguish between enveloping depression and an experience of 'feeling a bit depressed'. There must be very few people who never feel in the least bit depressed, but that is not to say that the rest are 'the victims of depression' or 'suffer from depression'. If you can speak of yourself as being 'out of sorts', 'a bit under the weather' or of having 'a touch of the blues' or 'that Monday morning feeling' you are not likely to have plumbed the depths of depression. For those who hit the bottom would find it difficult to speak so lightly of this experience. Some know what it is to battle with tears for weeks on end. Others, who feel every bit as deeply depressed as those who show it by their non-stop tears, are dry-eyed in their misery. And this 'dry-eyed misery' is just as blanketing and sapping as the tearful sort, though naturally it is not so easy to recognise it for what it is. But we need to remember that a sensitive soul who has to battle with ready tears is not necessarily a victim of depression.

Recognising that there are varying degrees and, as we shall see later, different kinds of depression, how can we account for the fact that some people never show any signs of depression and possibly feel depressed only very rarely, if ever, while others have to fight such a battle with it?

Temperament enters into this. Some optimists know next to nothing of real depression, but the pessimists tend to see the black side of everything. There are those who are upset by the least thing. An unkind look, a thoughtless word, a dish that didn't turn out right, a wrong turning, an interrupted morning, an arrangement falling through, a day of ceaseless rain (especially on holiday!), a very strong wind, a fall in the market, an unexpected bill, the feeling that their will has been crossed or that they were not noticed somewhere, or a book or 'plot' that ends on a sad note is quite enough to make some people feel thoroughly depressed and miserable. They readily forget all the good things of yesterday in their minor frustrations of today or their painful anticipation of the worst tomorrow. Some can get so depressed that life does not seem worth living any longer. They feel they are hopeless failures in themselves and unjustifiable burdens to others.

The phlegmatic are different. They are not so easily moved to any extreme. They feel little either of radiant, overflowing joy and spontaneous excitement or of dull, overpowering despair. They just go on quietly from day to day.

Environment enters into it. A tense atmosphere at home, due to jealousy, suspicion, fear or the behaviour of some selfish personalities in chronic maladjustment can make it much easier for the heavy hand of depression to lie on those shut in to such an environment. Some caged birds can sing. Others forget their song!

Bereavement, or some shattering experience, is a common cause of temporary and very understandable depression. It is desperately hard to be cheerful when you are cut off from somebody unspeakably dear to you. If you know they have gone to be with the Lord in a far better place (as Christians do) that makes the separation more bearable when you think of those who have passed on. But it doesn't make you miss them any the less, or dispel all heaviness of spirit, unless the loved one was very old, feeble and suffering. Few people who care and feel at all deeply can shrug off easily the loss of companion, guide, lover and friend, even though they know the separation is only temporary and they realise they have the Lord's Presence and help still with them.

Some go through a tough patch in middle years, while others have to face it in old age. 'Big factors in *advancing years,*'writes a Christian psychiatrist, 'may be loneliness, a sense of being unwanted, and the realisation that powers of body and mind are failing; the old can suffer very severe depression. So can foreign students, or foreign workers, and country

people obliged to live in cities.' Some unfortunate
people pass through a very long tunnel of depression,
when they dissolve into tears at the least difficulty
or find themselves weeping for nothing at all. The
Christians among them may know at the very same
time, paradoxically, an extraordinary, deep, underlying
peace, strangely out of keeping with the tears which
seem to be quite beyond their control.

One's general *state of health* also enters into it.
Marked depression may follow or be associated with
physical illness, e.g. influenza or after major surgery.
When people are physically well, and are getting
enough work, sleep and recreation, they generally find
it much easier to fight tendencies to depression. But we
must not only think of health in a general way. *There
are severe forms of depression which when correctly
diagnosed are very treatable illnesses.* Some of those so
affected were previously cheerful, sociable and outgoing personalities. Others had always been lacking in
the joy of living. Some were conscientious and
scrupulous, guilt-prone perfectionists; others were
fussy and overburdened like Martha. (See Luke
10:38-42.) These severe depressions may not lift for
long periods (months or even years) unless treated
medically. They are associated with lack of sleep, the
patient usually waking early. There is loss of interest
and initiative, difficulty in making decisions and a
sense of everything being a burden, especially in the
mornings. Ordinary daily tasks may appear as great
mountains of difficulty, rather than little chores to be
quickly got out of the way. There may be a lack of
spontaneity and vitality in action and conversation. It is
almost impossible to draw such people out of their
shells. Or there may be the other extreme – great
restlessness, agitation, apprehension and anxiety.
Their facial expressions betray their unhappiness.
Those who suffer from severe depression often blame

themselves for their condition. 'It's all my fault,' they say. They may develop delusions, false beliefs which usually are obviously untrue to those who know the sufferer but out of which he cannot be shaken by reasoning or argument. One sufferer may be deluded that he has caused extreme suffering or harm to others; another may be deluded that the doctor or some other person trying to help him or her in a professional capacity is in love with them. They may complain of physical symptoms and express fear of cancer or some other dread disease or unwarranted anxiety over their affairs. And they will frequently feel that they are the worst people in the world. Telling them, whether sharply or in a kindly way, to pull themselves together is no help to them at all. When they are really down they find it desperately hard, if not impossible, to believe anything at all. To them, life is grim, and the past is ruined beyond forgiveness or its disastrous effects are beyond repair. The present is meaningless. Their burdens are intolerable. The future is hopeless. They feel nobody understands them and nobody can help them. Death would be welcome. They ask themselves whether it is worth going on existing when all appears to dark and hopeless.

Anyone seeking to impress upon those suffering from this form of depression that the answer is spiritual is only likely to make matters worse. Prayer and encouragement from the Bible will not always provide a complete answer where medical help is needed and is available. There is no doubt that many have derived great benefit from electro-convulsive therapy (E.C.T.), some on more than one occasion. And while some patients may be forgetful or muddled for a little while following the treatment, burdens on the mind, which unfortunately could not previously be removed from their all-absorbing, dominating, central positions, are now lifted, and a more balanced and healthy perspective is regained. They are then more able to appreciate spiritual help.

There are certain drugs now available which can relieve many of these patients, though their selection requires expert knowledge. And we can look on drugs, rightly used, as God's gracious gifts. The raw materials are all of His providing, and the combination of these is due to wisdom which in His common grace He has given to mankind. All God's gifts can be abused, and so can these drugs. But a right use of them can bring relief and often open the door and windows of the mind to further gracious and helpful influences. It is wonderful to see the dull, unresponsive look of a sufferer gradually replaced by the warm, responsive look of someone who is able once more to face life normally and laugh again at things which are humorous.

What a priceless gift a sense of humour is! In some few it needs curbing. In most it needs cultivating. Many feel that their sanity has only been preserved on occasions by their sense of humour. In most non-Christians the sense of humour needs purifying, a process which cannot be experienced, generally speaking, apart from the person turning with all their heart to Christ. A cleansed sense of humour is one of the by-products of genuine Christian conversion.

But the counsel to 'cultivate a sense of humour' is no more the complete answer than the useless advice to 'pull yourself together and snap out of it', when depression is due to physical or mental illness. We need then what God can give us through medical help. And there are times when those who suffer from this form of depression are incapable of appreciating any spiritual help offered to them until they have received medical help.

Some depressions are not illnesses in the same sense as the severe depressions just referred to. The reasons for the most common forms of depression are many and varied. Some find severe indigestion depressing; others hay-fever or some other mild chronic affliction, or any bout of illness. Others find sympathy for their condition even more depressing than the sickness itself! Not being able to sleep properly is depressing. Failure, or coming short of the standard you have set for yourself, is depressing. An impaired relationship with someone dear to you, or someone you would love to be friendly with, is depressing. You must have heard the saying, 'Most newspapers make depressing reading.' To be tied down to work which you feel does not do justice to your capabilities, training or upbringing is depressing. To be disappointed in love is depressing. And what depths of depression some can sink into! Some of us have no idea how black things can look to the more sensitive. What is a trifling difficulty to one person can be mountainous − almost an overwhelming catastrophe − to somebody hypersensitive. And sympathy will help such people (as it does the vast majority of people always), where scorn, ridicule or reproach will only hurt them more and make them more than ever depressed. There may be times when we should seek in a gentle way to help the depressed not to take themselves too seriously. They are making real progress when they can smile at themselves!

People suffering from severe anxiety states may also become depressed, but their depression is less all-absorbing and varies with circumstances. These people are more likely to blame their environment than themselves. Some depressions would appear more obviously to be reactions to circumstances, very often in the sensitive, over-conscientious worrier. They see a job needs doing, and if nobody else is offering to do it they must get it done. They worry a lot about it once they have taken it on. They can see they already have too much on their plate, and they cannot do any of it as well as they would like. To their deep disappointment, they see their former duties suffering, too. The more they attempt, the less they achieve. Anxiety mounts up and efficiency falls away. And, too often, there is no sign of anybody coming forward to relieve them. They don't want to make a fuss about it, but is there nobody who can see what a state they are in? How much more can they stand? They don't want to give in. They don't want to let anybody down. They are in a vicious circle.

Their depression is usually worse in the evening. They have great difficulty in getting off to sleep. They just lie there worrying, turning things over and over again in their minds — what they have said or done, failed to say or do; what somebody else has said, done or forgotten to do, or worse still refused to do; what must be done tomorrow or very soon or else... They do not blame themselves for everything. They can often find some causes outside themselves why things have gone wrong. Someone has let them down. The more they like that person, the more hurt and depressed they are.

Their mood can be shifted very quickly. An encouraging letter, a phone call from a friend, a surprise visit from somebody they think highly of, and you could never guess how troubled they were only last night. They respond very readily to human warmth. It soon lifts them out of the pit of depression, 'brings them out of themselves'. Electro-convulsive therapy is unlikely to help people suffering from this sort of depression, though sometimes those suffering from anxiety reactions or other neurotic states are helped by psychotherapy or modern drugs. Those who are suffering from *persistent* anxiety states should not hesitate to seek medical advice. Many anxiety states (feeling 'all tensed-up' or 'strung-up') which occur for the first time in middle or later life are in fact severe depressions, with associated anxiety and apprehension or dread of something that is going to happen or go wrong. But the patient may not describe himself as being depressed, and he may only appear overburdened with personal or business worries, or obsessed with ideas about really serious ill-health. Such may require modern anti-depressant drugs and, in some cases, a brief course of electric treatment. The Christian however, especially if the problem causing him to feel depressed concerns his spiritual life, has another answer. When great saints have known depression they have found relief in spreading out the matter before God in unhurried, quiet prayer on their own. Some need the fellowship of others in prayer to help them get 'on top' again.

The prophet Elijah knew what it was to be terribly depressed. 'I am no better than my fathers. I don't want to live a day longer. Let me die,' he said, sheltering from the grilling sun under a juniper tree. For years, almost single-handed, he had stood up to the wicked King Ahab with splendid courage. He had defied the prophets of Baal with magnificent faith. But that woman Jezebel was after his blood, and reaction had set in. Courage and faith, peace and hope, had evaporated. He had, literally, to run away. When his weary legs could not carry him a yard further, he said, 'What is the use of going on? That woman will get me in the end. She will have me hounded to death. Surely it is better for me to die now.' God met him in his depression and graciously lifted him out of it. There was vital work for him to do yet. And he had more allies than he realised – God's 'seven thousand'. And God saw that he needed restful sleep and nourishing food before he could do anything more in His service. (See I Kings 19.)

The prophet Jeremiah knew what it was to be depressed. If only he had some encouraging news to bring to the people! If only he could say fine things in the name of God that would make them grateful for his messages! The Lord had thrust him into the ministry of a prophet. But he found his work shot through with frustrations, trials and disappointments for which he had never bargained. Surely if he was serving and obeying God everything should go absolutely right. Should it? When did God ever promise skies ever blue, roses without thorns, joy without tears? Jeremiah felt depressed because the more he passed on God's message, the more he was ridiculed. But the Lord's answer was, 'He who has My word, let him speak My word faithfully.' And what messages God gave His servant after that, assuring him he was loved with everlasting love (31:3), and revealing through him the terms of His new covenant or 'arrangement' (31: 31-34).

David, described in the New Testament as a man after God's own heart, knew what depression was. Who, chased from pillar to post as he was, would not have felt depressed at times? 'Why are you cast down, O my soul? and why are you disquieted within me?' But he called on his soul within him even in the midst of the depression, 'Hope on in God: for I shall yet praise Him, who is the health of my countenance, and my God' (Ps. 42 and 43).

Even Paul, the greatest missionary leader of the early church, the apostle of the Gentiles, knew his hours of depression. He was not depressed because of any uncomfortable experience he was going through himself. God had taught him to glory in his own infirmities, troubles he had to face, persecutions and other disagreeable circumstances he had to endure, for it was in the midst of these very things that the power of God rested upon him. But he was depressed, heavy in heart, burdened in mind and spirit, when things went wrong for his young children in the Faith; when his enemies came to pervert their simple faith in the Lord Jesus; when unscrupulous men aspired to leadership;

when shameful failure overtook young converts; when young churches were rocked; when it looked for a while as though Satan was stronger than God and the truth might not prevail. Yet Paul can speak of his God as the God who comforts those who are cast down (II Cor. 1:3,4,8-10; 2:13; 7:6).

If heaviness of heart can in any way be identified with depression, then our Lord Jesus knew this experience, for example when He wept over Jerusalem. But – and what a big but – His heartache was not for Himself but for others. No Christian would dream of suggesting that His heavy, broken-hearted feeling was sinful. He knew no sin. He did no sin. In Him was no sin. Self-centred concern is quite different. We need to distinguish between things that are different.

If a great saint like Paul, the great prophets of the Old Testament times, and a Reformation hero like Luther, could feel depressed at times, is it to be wondered at that many lesser folk like ourselves, Christians though we may be, should feel depressed at times? It has often been said that God never did anything with a discouraged man, and we must not overlook the fact that discouragement is a favourite weapon of the devil. Nor should we belittle the splendid attitude summed up in the words, 'I refuse to be discouraged; I will only praise.' There is a depression, however, which is nothing less than sinful, an expression of our self-centred, rebellious nature, as, for example, when our depression is due to hurt pride. But, as we have seen, not all depression is sinful, being sometimes due to illness, either as a symptom or as a consequence of that illness dragging on and recovery still seeming such a long way off. 'Hope deferred makes the heart sick' (Prov. 13:12). Such depression is not to be traced to our personal sin, though had sin not been introduced into the world, there would have been neither sickness nor depression.

A Christian may well ask at this point, 'What about the depression that comes with genuine conviction of sin?' By conviction of sin we mean an awareness of guilt, of having pulled away from God and His will as expressed in the Bible or imprinted on our conscience. Whether we are Christians or not yet Christians, true conviction of sin is something that is always distressing and can be depressing. And when we meet someone who is under *this* depression we should not try to lift it as a symptom to be treated in isolation. We should pray that this particular depression should drive them *in despair of themselves* to the Lord Jesus, for forgiveness and peace. None but He can take away their sin and guilt. None but He can rightly lift the accompanying depression. His invitation and promise still hold good, 'Come unto Me, all you who are weary and heavily burdened, and I will give you rest' (Matt. 11:28).

While what is said above obviously applies to those who experience real conviction of sin, Christian psychiatrists tell us there is also a pathological guilt often associated with depression felt by over-scrupulous people, including some Christians, who suffer from obsessions. These hypersensitive introverts may feel guilt concerning relatively trivial offences about which they can do nothing, or, in extreme cases, over *imagined* offences built up by an over-active imagination. They have earnestly sought forgiveness yet still feel 'guilty' and depressed. Their trouble is not spiritual. But there are those whose trouble really is spiritual. At the root of all their depression is either failure to trust Christ for His forgiveness or failure to put right, where this is possible, the wrongs that are on their consciences. Drugs and reassuring words are no substitute for apologies and restitution. The cure, like the malady, is spiritual. (See Matt. 5:23,24) To get right with someone we have wronged may be costly to our human pride. Some find it harder to confess their sin to a fellow human-being whom they can see than to the God whom they cannot see. But the relief that follows the reconciliation far outweighs the cost. And peace and joy come back to our hearts even if attempts to sort things out are brushed aside and our sincere apologies dismissed as insincere. God knows our heart.

What should we do, then, if we find ourselves depressed? We should seek to discover the reason, or combination of reasons, and when it is spiritual apply the specific remedy to which God's Word points us. Sometimes it may take another human personality to illuminate God's truth to us and help us to apply it ourselves. At other times, perhaps most times, we may 'get through on our own'. But we should never be too proud or too humble to ask for help when we need it. The God and Father of our Lord Jesus Christ is a God who has the answer for His children when they are depressed. He has His own ways of lifting them out of their depression, strengthening their faith and hope and love.

At this point I ought to reiterate that not all depression is due to some spiritual disorder. But when it is, we can only expect the depression to lift when the disorder is dealt with on a spiritual basis. Symptoms generally vanish with the healing of disease, but with spiritual disorders they may persist for some time after the disease has, by God's grace, been dealt with. If we went slowly down many steps into the valley of depression we should not necessarily expect to take one long leap out of it. There may have to be steps up again. And the joy of our salvation may be slow in coming back.

Now let us look at *clues which may help us to cope* with some of the specific reasons for depression.

(1) When cast down or depressed because of *our own sin and failures* there are three strands in the answer set before us in the Bible, God's Word. (a) We must turn

to the God who sent His Son to die for our sin, and confess it honestly to Him, and renounce it; we must go that way no more. (b) We must lay hold of the promise of cleansing and forgiveness for the sake of Him who suffered for man's sin. 'If we confess our sins, He is faithful and just to forgive us our sins and to cleanse us from all unrighteousness' (I John 1:7-10; 2:1,2). (c) We must praise Him that He is listening to our earnest cry and trust Him to restore to us the joy of our salvation. The saved cannot lose their salvation, but they can, and many do, lose the joy of it (Ps.51:1-15).

> *My sin is black, I know it, Lord,*
> *   But You for me have died;*
> *Cleanse me, that joy may be restored,*
> *   And keep me by Your side.*

(2) When depressed because of our sense of *weakness and inadequacy* we may find the way of deliverance from this in God's Word. His Word assures us that His grace is sufficient for every man and woman who trusts in Him. His strength is made perfect in our weakness, and only in our weakness. Instead of complaining and even despairing because of our conscious weakness, we should thank Him for everything that drives us in our weakness to His feet (II Cor. 12:9,10).

(3) If we are depressed because of our *disappointed hopes* we may find the way out of our depression through grasping the truth that 'no good thing will He withhold from those who walk uprightly' (Ps. 84:11). If what we had set our hearts on was really good for us the Lord would have seen to it that we should have it. Perhaps the time is not yet. Maybe in His time it will come. 'As for God, His way is perfect.' It is for us to 'walk uprightly', i.e. to keep our eyes on Him each step we take, moment by moment, day by day.

(4) If depression is due to *fear of the future* we may

find an answer in the words of command and promise in Luke 12:4-7, Luke 21:25-28 and Philippians 3:20,21. 'Fear not those who kill the body and after that have no more that they can do...you are of more value than many sparrows...the very hairs of your head are numbered.' 'Upon the earth distress of nations, with perplexity...men's hearts failing them for fear of those things which are coming upon the earth...When you see these things begin to pass, lift up your heads, your redemption is drawing nigh.' 'Our citizenship is in heaven; from whence also we wait for a Saviour, the Lord Jesus Christ: who shall fashion anew the body of our humiliation, that it may be conformed to the body of His glory, according to the working whereby He is able even to subject all things unto Himself' (R.V.). And right up to that very moment He has everything absolutely under His control for His children, so that we can confidently say with Ryland:

> *Plagues and death around me fly,*
> *Till He bids I cannot die;*
> *Not a single shaft can hit*
> *Till the God of love sees fit.*

(5) If depression is due to *loneliness and the sense that we have been forsaken*, either by our fellow-Christians, our families or our God, we may find the answer in Hebrews 13:5,6,8: 'He hath said, I will never leave thee, nor forsake thee. So that we may boldly say, the Lord is my helper, and I will not fear what man shall do unto me...Jesus Christ (is) the same yesterday,'– for Paul, Augustine, Calvin, Luther, Wesley, Whitfield, George Muller, Hudson Taylor, Geoffrey Bull, Isobel Kuhn – 'and today,' – for me and every other born-again believer, whatever his race or place – 'and for ever.' God still comforts those who are cast down because they lack the fellowship of their beloved

fellow-workers (II Cor. 2:13 and 7:6). 'This is the word of a perfect Gentleman,' wrote David Livingstone in the heart of Africa, as he meditated on our Lord's words: 'Lo, I am with you alway, even unto the end of the world.' God can do anything but fail us. God cannot lie. He cannot break His word. It was only when John Bunyan's Christian and Hopeful remembered the promises of God that they escaped from Giant Despair's dungeon in Doubting Castle! As we lay hold of His promises and plead them before His throne, He who is faithful to His promises will lift us. (See Ps. 27:10; 71:18,19; Isa. 49:14-16.)

(6) If we are depressed because of *difficult circumstances in which we find ourselves* we may find the answer in Romans 8:28. It is not the whole truth that ninety-nine out of a hundred things work together for the good of God's children. The truth is that *all* things, including the fruit of our own blunders and stupidity, sinfulness and ignorance, including the things we cry to God for deliverance from (as Paul did in II Corinthians 12:8), work together for good to those who love God. Faith must take hold of this word and deliberately commit the difficult, depressing circumstances to Him who is able to subdue all things unto Himself, that having sifted us as wheat He may bring us through with a strengthened faith. We may cast all our anxieties, burdens, problems, cares, worries, upon Him, for it does matter to Him about us (I Pet. 5:7). He could not care more.

(7) If we are depressed because of *the failure, the apparently inconsistent, disappointing behaviour of other Christians towards us,* we may find clues to the answer in Luke 22:61 and John 21:20-22. We have a High Priest before God on high who knows what it is to be touched deeply in this area. Judas, treasurer of the disciples, betrayed Him. Simon Peter, of the 'inner circle' of disciples, denied that he knew Him. All His

disciples forsook Him and fled. Even John, the beloved disciple, failed to speak up for Him when he might have done, though he came back and stood near His feet at the cross. Whatever others may do to us, no matter how depressing those things may be, our Lord's words should come ringing clear over all the waves of depression, 'What is that to you? follow you Me.' He knows all about it. He remembers how it hurts (Ps. 69:9,20).

(8) If we find ourselves depressed by *the failure of other Christians not to grow* we may find the answer in Philippians 1:6 and Hebrews 13:20,21. Those who have made only an outward profession of conversion under the pressure of a highly emotional atmosphere can hardly be expected to grow. Where there is no spiritual life we must not look for spiritual growth. But there are those who have been quickened by God's Word, genuinely converted, who get bogged down. And it is indeed depressing to see some who made such a bright profession of faith on first turning to Christ, making such little headway. This is generally due to failure in the daily discipline of Christian living, Bible-reading, prayer, fellowship and witness, or failure to depend on the indwelling Holy Spirit. It is more depressing still to see some who were born again many years ago still babes in understanding or unbalanced in doctrine, unused to praying with one another, apparently un-concerned about people around them drifting into eternity altogether unprepared. The state of these immature Christians grieves the heart of their Heaven-ly Father, and yet He does not give them up. It is for us to go on caring and praying and not to condemn, even though they drive us to tears at times. We must look to Him for them, not to them for Him.

(9) If we are depressed for *fears for the future of Christ's Church* we may find the answer in Matthew 16:18, 18:20 and 28:19,20. Christ is still among His

believing people on earth, unseen yet gloriously real. He will go on building His Church until the last living stone is in place. The fellowship of His people is not ended at the point of death, though those still living on earth are not meant to seek to establish contact with those who have passed on. The gates of Hades, the place of departed spirits, are under Christ's control. And no scheme worked out in hell against Christ's Church shall finally prevail over it. Christ has promised His abiding presence right up to the very end of the age. And He cannot fail, for He is God. Nor can His Church be destroyed, whatever religious institutions may vanish, for He needs her on earth, to the very end, as His salt, His light, His body through which He can express His will.

(10) If we get depressed because of *fierce temptations or prolonged testings* we may find great help in I Corinthians 10:13; James 1:12; Jude 24,25; and Hebrews 7:25. God will not allow us to be tempted beyond recovery or tested beyond our strength. He gauges the strength of the temptation or testing before He allows it to hit us. He limits the power of His enemy and ours to assail us, as the early chapters of Job so vividly illustrate. What is more, in addition to the joy and relief of overcoming, there are strong incentives to withstand temptation or endure testing. Does not our victory please the Christ who suffered so much for us? And has not the Lord promised a crown to those who come victoriously through fierce testings and temptations? And we may prove in our own experience that He is able to save to the uttermost extent all those who are in the habit of coming unto God through Him. He is ever alive to our need, quick to put in a word for us, to step in on our behalf and deal with things which have got beyond us. So when we get depressed by the strength of trying situations — perhaps oppressed would be more correct than depressed in this context

– or the attraction of thoughts, words and deeds which are wrong, let us come boldly to the Throne of Grace, that we may find grace to help in such a time of need.

(11) When we feel depressed because of general *mental pressure* we may find a clue to the answer in Isaiah 26:3; Philippians 4:4-7; and II Corinthians 1:8-10. God will keep in perfect peace the person whose mind, memory and imagination is stayed on Him. This means deliberately turning our thoughts towards His faithfulness and His promises, and refusing to go on thinking about the same old things again and again; for that process gets us absolutely nowhere and only digs a deeper groove in an over-active imagination, an overwrought conscience or an over-worked memory. Turn your eyes upon Jesus. Listen to Him. 'Lie still and let Him mould you.' 'Be still, and know that I am God' (Ps. 46:1,10,11).

But, as we thought earlier, we must not leave people with the impression that succumbing to mental pressure is *always* due to spiritual failure. Yet such collapse is sometimes one of the consequences of the barrenness which can easily blight the life of a Christian who takes far too little time for rest, prayer, meditation and private Bible study (i.e. just feeding, as distinct from preparing for meetings). There are too many over-rushed, tense, harassed children of God. How can such help being irritable at home? 'Come ye yourselves apart...and rest a while' is not an invitation the Lord has withdrawn from circulation. And He Himself spent nights in prayer.

> Drop Thy still dews of quietness
>   Till all our strivings cease;
> Take from our souls the strain and stress
> And let our ordered lives confess
>   The beauty of Thy peace.

(12) There are very likely to be times in the life of a Christian when depression is due to a *satanic attack*. Whereas the devil blinds unbelievers to their spiritual needs, he tries to get Christians thoroughly introverted and to believe that all their troubles are due to spiritual failure.

God never nags, but He does convict of sin. His purpose in convicting us is to bring us to repentance (Rom. 2:4), a thorough-going revulsion from ourselves and our failure, a true sorrow for the hurt it has given to God and others, and a firm determination that by the grace of God we shall pass no more that way. True repentance goes hand in hand with renewed faith, as we lay hold afresh upon the benefits of the death of the Lord Jesus. 'If any man sin, we have an advocate with the Father, Jesus Christ the righteous: and He is the propitiation for our sins' (I John 2:1,2). But whereas God convicts, His conviction is always specific, not vague, and He always lifts the sense of conviction when we repent and turn afresh in brokenness to Calvary.

The devil, on the other hand, nags at memory and conscience and imagination, and keeps on and on at us about things for which we have claimed God's forgiveness and cleansing. This can be very depressing. We need to remember that the devil is the 'accuser of the brethren'. His is the mastermind behind most spiritual discouragement. He plots to keep people from Christ. He schemes to make Christians useless. He seeks to belittle some and puff up others, according to whether they are naturally inclined to faint-heartedness or pride. The devil will do his utmost to keep us looking at ourselves and our difficulties and weaknesses. He will do all he can to keep our eyes off Christ and His finished work for us on the cross and His unfinished work on the throne. We may find the answer to satanically imposed depression in such Scriptures as Psalm 25:15:

'My eyes are ever toward the Lord; for He shall pluck my feet out of the net (spread by the enemy).'

Isaiah 59:19:

'When the enemy shall come in like a flood, the Spirit of the Lord shall lift up a standard against him.'

I Peter 5:8,9:

'Your adversary the devil, as a roaring lion, walketh about, seeking whom he may devour: whom resist stedfast in the faith.'

and Revelation 12:11:

'They overcame him (the accuser) by the blood of the Lamb, and by the word of their testimony; and they loved not their lives unto the death.'

When Satan tempts me to despair,
  And tells me of the guilt within,
Upward I look, and see Him there
  Who made an end of all my sin.

While some bouts of depression may be due to sin or overwork and overworry, others are due to a nervous and introspective disposition which spiritual treatment may help to mitigate but does not overcome. The Christian worker needs wisdom to know where a condition goes beyond his powers to help it, where medical care and attention is the answer. If after prayerful and sympathetic application of Scriptural truth by a mature and experienced Christian worker the depression fails to lift it is usually wise to seek medical aid. The converse is true. Thank God for the doctors who know where medical treatment has reached its limits and spiritual help is needed to take the patient further. In many situations today doctors and Christian workers are co-operating harmoniously for the benefit of the same patient, but there is plenty of room for improvement in this field.

A final word to Christian readers. It is remarkable how often depression lifts when we make, mentally or on paper, a list of our blessings and begin to thank God for them. This should not surprise us, for His word says, 'Whoever offers praise glorifies Me (i.e. gives God the place of honour due to Him in our mind and life) and makes a way whereby I may go on showing him the salvation (deliverance, saving strength) of God', as Psalm 50:23 may be translated. Praise makes a way.

Some periods of depression, as following bereavement of someone very precious, may defy praise, but these are the exception rather than the rule.

Martin Luther came home greatly depressed one day. Things were never easy for the great German Reformer. But at this time the complex accumulation of difficulties seemed simply appalling. Foes were pressing him hard and friends were failing him wholesale. He felt overwhelmed, quite unable to cope. But why did his wife greet him clothed in black from head to feet?

'I have worse news than yours,' she said.

'Worse than mine!' he exclaimed incredulously.

'Yes,' answered Catherine. 'God is dead.'

'God dead!' he shouted. 'No!'

And, reaching eagerly for his lyre, he played and sang with intense feeling his own great battle hymn,

A safe stronghold our God is still
  A trusty shield and weapon;
He'll keep us safe through all the ill
  Which hath us now o'ertaken.

The English poet Cowper was subject to deep depression of the kind that in our day might well have responded to medical treatment. Once he hired a man to drive him to the River Ouse so that he might throw himself in and end it all. A dense fog came down and the coachman got completely lost. He groped his way up to a front door. It was William Cowper's own. Small wonder that the poet sat down in his home and wrote,

God moves in a mysterious way...

Ye fearful saints, fresh courage take!
   The clouds ye so much dread
Are big with mercy and will break
   In blessings on your head.

Blind unbelief is sure to err
   And scan His work in vain;
God is His own interpreter
   And He will make it plain.

Even on his death-bed Cowper experienced deep depression, but those watching saw such a look of relief on his face just before he died. The doors were opening. His burden was gone. He was comforted.

When people we know get depressed let us give them all the help we can, that they may overcome it. When we ourselves get depressed let us turn to the Lord, seeking His wisdom to find the cause and then His help that we may be delivered from it. One very good reason why we may confidently look to Him for deliverance is this: He knows that while we are depressed we are not able to fulfill our desire to be effective Christian witnesses.

'All those words which were written long ago are meant to teach us today; that when we read in the

Scriptures of the endurance of men and of all the help that God gave them in those days, we may be encouraged to go on hoping in our own time. May the God who inspires men to endure, and gives them a Father's care, give you a mind united towards one another because of your common loyalty to Jesus Christ. And then, as one man, you will sing from the heart the praises of God the Father of our Lord Jesus Christ. So open your hearts to one another as Christ has opened His heart to you, and God will be glorified.'

'May the God of Hope fill you with joy and peace in your faith, that by the power of the Holy Spirit, your whole life and outlook may be radiant with hope' (Rom. 15:4-7, 13 J.B. Phillips).

A final word to someone who is not yet a committed Christian. It may be as difficult as it is important for you to grasp the fact that one reason for depression is conviction of sin. This conviction of sin is a sense of guilt and need, a sense of being all wrong, having broken God's laws, being rebellious at heart, having hurt God and deserving His condemnation. God fastens this conviction on those He is calling to Himself. Sometimes they feel its full strength only after they have come to Him as sinners. We may try to shake it off by flinging ourselves into a whirl of social activity, or by dashing from one religious service to another, or by throwing ourselves into the splendid task of trying to help those less fortunate than ourselves. Giving ourselves to helping others often proves to be an excellent antidote for those already right with God, but it is no substitute for getting right with God.

And for those who have never found Christ personally, *this* depression is a symptom, not a medical disease. But as we thought earlier, it is no use trying to treat the symptom in isolation. The disease is sin. And only as sin in our life is dealt with can we satisfactorily get rid of the depression that generally comes with a sense of guilt. A sense of guilt includes an awareness that I am rightly exposed to the penalties of laws I have broken; it doesn't stop short at disappointment with myself, my inability to control myself, my failure to arrive. At this point there is nothing in the world more relevant than the Christian Good News. (See Rom. 1:16; 10:12.)

God not only made man. He made the rules for His creatures and attached the penalties without consulting us. In other words, God has laid down the law. We have all broken God's laws. We deserve to be banished from Him for ever. But God loves us, wretched, self-centred lawbreakers though we are. And God sent His Son to take the lawbreaker's place under the condemnation due to him. The punishment due to man's sin was poured out upon the sinless head of the Son of God when He hung upon a wooden cross outside the walls of old Jerusalem nearly two thousand years ago – at the turning-point of history. He died, forsaken by men and God. But His death was not the end. On the third day He rose from the dead. And He is alive today. The risen Christ can hear my cry for help. He can meet my needs. And if I turn from my sins, and my own way of living my life, to Him who died under the unspeakable burden of a world's sin, I can and will find full and free forgiveness at His expense. This is God's arrangement. And in it the Son sees eye to eye with the Father. The Father gave His Son. The Son gave Himself. And there is *no other way* for the sinner to be forgiven (Acts 4:12).

> *There was no other good enough*
> *To pay the price of sin;*
> *He only could unlock the gate*
> *Of heaven, and let us in.*

When we find His forgiveness, and know that we are going to heaven when we die, the depression due to a guilty conscience need not stay. For then 'we have peace with God through our Lord Jesus Christ'. (See Romans 5:1-11.) Have you this peace? Or are you yet unforgiven? Seek the Lord while He may be found. Call upon Him to save you while He is near, while you have life and breath and opportunity. This is the day of salvation. Tomorrow may be too late. You will learn to thank God for the unhappiness and sense of help-lessness that drove you despairing of any other help, to the feet of the Lord Jesus. He cares for you. He could not care more. And He can cope. Prove Him! But don't imagine that you can evade Him indefinitely. He is absolutely inescapable. If we do not trust Him as our living Saviour in this life we must face Him as our final Judge in the life of the world to come. (See Acts 10:42,43; 17:30,31.) God has appointed Him Judge of the living and the dead. But to Him give all the prophets witness that *whosoever* believes in Him shall receive the forgiveness of sins through His name. And those who find Him and His forgiveness find a peace that replaces this particular depression, a peace which the world cannot give and cannot take away, a peace which passes all understanding. This peace may be yours. (See John 14:1,27; 16:33; Philippians 4:4-7.)

For those who would like a much fuller treatment of the subject let me commend *Spiritual Depression, its causes and cure*, by Dr. Martyn Lloyd-Jones, published by Pickering and Inglis.

Chapter 8

TEMPTATION

Temptation hits us all. The first person in human history to be tempted was a woman. A charming personality with a brilliant mind suggested to her that her Creator God had been unfair in keeping from her what was obviously for her highest good. Doubts about God's wisdom and goodness were slipped into her mind alongside the suggestion that He couldn't really mean to carry out His threat of punishment for disobedience. The woman wavered in her loyalty. She failed to consult her husband. She fell.

The second person whose temptation is recorded was a man, the woman's husband. He too fell. And his fall was more serious, because he wasn't fooled as his wife had been. He went wrong with his eyes wide open. And his disobedience has had devastating consequences. For the thousands of years of human history since, all men and women have been born with a rebellious twist to their human nature. The marks of that fall can be seen in us all.

Mind you, there has been one exception. Only one! The only person in history who wasn't 'fallen' and warped by human sin lived in a small enemy-occupied land between Egypt and Syria nearly twenty centuries ago. Certain things mark Him off from the rest of us. His conception was miraculous, His birth was unique. His life was spotless. His death was bloody, violent and awful, but it was an atoning death. He died that men and women who are at enmity with God might become at one with God. Reconciled! And His resurrection from the dead was triumphant. One day He will come again to judge the living and the dead.

Yes, Jesus Christ was different. So different from us.

But even He was tempted. He was tempted, but He did not fall.

You see, *temptation is not sin.* Toying with some particular temptation and wondering if you can get away with it is sin. If you would dare to do whatever it is you are tempted to do but did not for the fear of punishment or other unpleasant consequences if you were found out, you have fallen for that temptation already in your heart. The inward stain of it is already on you. But if you fight the thing because you know it is wrong, then no matter how fiercely the temptation has stabbed you, no stain is left on your conscience.

THERE ARE VARIETIES OF TEMPTATION

All men are tempted, but not all are tempted in the same way. By the time you are twenty-one you should know what your particular temptations are, the usual trail that leads up to your coming a cropper. This also means that you should know what you should avoid if you are not to fall, what you need to be specially alert to.

Doubting God's love

Some people lose what faith they have in a good God when something goes wrong in the life of someone dear to them. Perhaps they pray for the speedy healing of a loved one and God doesn't seem to be listening. 'Perhaps He's not there after all? Perhaps He doesn't care enough about us? Perhaps He can't cope?' How many youngsters harden off into what they call atheism because of what they think is 'unanswered prayer'? They don't realise that 'no' is an answer, even if it is not the answer we want. 'Yes, but not yet' is another answer. And 'yes, but not your way' is still another answer. Happy is the person who comes to a God who is to be relied on to give the very best to those who ask, a God who is bigger than a resourceful but easy-to-be-persuaded Giver of what we think is best!

Doubting God's existence

'You tell me who made God before you open your mouth to go any further,' said an angry Welsh lady during an interesting train journey. 'All that fairy story stuff about feeding five thousand out of a picnic basket. Utter nonsense! Only a fool would believe it,' she shouted. 'If He does exist, why doesn't He do something about Northern Ireland?' she went on.

It is perfectly true that there are plenty of things in the world around us to make people wonder if there is such a person as a good God, or if He is 'there' and is good, whether He has the power to do anything about it. 'Evolution has debunked your Creator God' was her parting shot. The terrible things happening every day can have opposite consequences. Some people are driven to despair. Others, in search of 'something' are driven to read the Bible.

Self-centredness

Everyone notices and dislikes self-centredness in other people. But most of us are not aware of how self-centred we ourselves can be! Yet when we are thoughtless about the needs, wishes and interests of others, and involve them in unnecessary inconvenience we show how self-centred we really are. So often we fail to do to others what we would like them to do to us, and do to them what we would hate anyone to do to us. Time and again we give in to the subtle temptation to be self-centred. 'What is there in this for me?' 'How can I get my own way in this?' 'How can I bring them all round to my way of thinking about that holiday?'

Questions like these motivate us far more often than most of us realise.

Dishonesty and Untruthfulness

In our still permissive society it is terribly easy to collect our 'perks' without thinking for a moment that we are being dishonest. Collective ownership (nationalised industries) used to make it easier to feel, 'Well, it's mine to start with anyway, so why shouldn't I take it home?' or 'Why should I pay if the chap isn't around?' Shop-lifting has reached alarming proportions. Factories are losing no end of material designed for export. Our national economic outlook would be remarkably different if everybody, including those in management, had given an honest day's work for a good day's wage throughout the past five years, and filled in time-sheets honestly. There are many people, who wouldn't dream of being dishonest with property, who cannot be counted on to tell the truth. A quick lie to boost our image, or to cover up a difficulty, comes so easily. Mind you, not every inaccurate statement is to be branded as a downright lie. Some people's memories fail so quickly. The essence of a lie is the intention to deceive.

Covetousness and Jealousy

Covetousness has more to do with things than with people. 'If I sell one washing-machine in that road, I can guarantee I will sell one to every house,' said a salesman in Berkshire. What about compact discs, the very latest hi-fi? or some other status symbol? Covetousness has become one of our great national sins. It is all too easy to get caught up in materialism, and feel 'we must get one too!'

Jealousy has more to do with people than with

things. How many friendships and even family relationships have been ruined by jealousy? Is the real reason why we have a down on someone simply that we are secretly jealous of them? Jealousy is one of the most insidious and destructive of human temptations. Small wonder that it has been called 'the green-eyed monster'!

Indiscipline

Any old excuse for putting off what we ought to be getting on with! Is it tiredness that keeps us from church on Sunday mornings or is it simply that we have not organised our time properly during the week, or not disciplined ourselves enough to go to bed at the right time? One of my friends often speaks of the last hour of the evening as 'the devil's hour', when so many dither, instead of making a determined effort to get to bed at a reasonable time. Urgent things can so easily crowd out the really important ones. Self-discipline should be admired, not scorned!

Pride and Snobbishness

Some who have had better opportunities for education than their parents are tempted to despise them for their ignorance or lack of culture. Do we look down our nose at the rest of the family? Or do we think that because someone belongs to an older generation they don't know a thing? Maybe we are good with our hands, and are tempted to despise those who lack our skills or our opportunities. Maybe we are particularly bright and are tempted to despise the less intelligent. Have we no time for those we think are 'thick'?

Bad Temper

This shows itself in more than one way. Some are more tempted than others to 'lose their cool'. They flare up at the slightest thing that upsets them. And they can give a very uncomfortable half-hour to someone who is not able to hit back with the same vigour or venom. Better to live in a small flat in peace than in a large house with a brawling man or woman, says the wise man in the Book of Proverbs. Some people who would not dream of 'blowing their top' withdraw into themselves and sulk. You never know where you are with them! They can stay irritable and resentful for such a long time! It isn't all that easy to know when it is safe to approach them again. At least the person who can't keep his cool usually gets it over fairly quickly, and is back to normal again as if nothing had ever happened.

Fear

Are you worried as you think about the future? Very few people are never afraid. Most fear is a form of self-love. Fear of what people would think of him or do to him made Peter, one of the very first disciples of Jesus Christ, deny that he even knew Him. Fear has kept many from handing their lives over completely to Jesus Christ, as if He would lead those He loves into a life of misery! Worry is chronic fear. Fear continually given in to becomes a state of anxiety. Fear cripples. Fear stunts. Fear distorts. 'For a short time I was crippled with fear about something happening to my husband while my children were young,' confessed a middle-aged mother. That kind of fear denotes lack of trust in the goodness and power of God. Fear can be so absorbing that you cannot concentrate on what you should be doing. Is giving in to fear, the fear of disease, or bereavement, or the unknown future, your constant temptation? If so, Psalm 34 could be a great help to you.

Despair

Most people find there are times when they want to pack in a job that is thoroughly boring, quit their course of studies, or even clear off from their troubled home. Have you ever thought, 'I wish I could go to sleep for three years, and only wake up when it's all sorted out'?

It is just possible that you are under such pressure, that recently the thought has been going through your mind, 'Shall I end it all?' At some stage or another a surprising number of people are tempted to commit suicide. In Japan alone, 60,000 died in this way in one year, nearly half of them students who had failed their exams. They felt they must atone for their failure, because to them success was the ultimate good, and failure the unforgiveable sin.

Lust

Sexual desire is natural. It only becomes sinful when misdirected or given scope at the wrong time. The Creator's plan is that sexual experience should belong to marriage. There should be no sex without responsibility. Many are kept from promiscuity who have no respect for the Creator or His plans. The fear of VD or of AIDS keeps them from gratifying their lusts in the loveless embrace of a prostitute or someone just wanting more 'fun'. Others are kept in the hour of temptation by their high views of marriage. They want to bring a pure, uncontaminated body to a life-partner whose self-discipline has matched their own.

But many people find what they see and hear all

around them in our still too-permissive society makes it
hard for them to stop at just appreciating face and
figure, just admiring. There is strong temptation to go
further, especially when the beat is strong, or the
weather particularly warm or the atmosphere relaxing.
Isn't everybody doing it? They think contraception has
solved all their serious problems. They don't realise
how much guilt, insecurity, bitterness and disillusion-
ment follow the breaking of the Maker's rules. For
God's laws are none other than the Maker's rules for
harmonious living, with ourselves and others. The vast
majority of us are attracted to the opposite sex. But
some have natural tendencies the other way: homosexual tendencies. A few are so cool and academic that
they can think of attractive members of the opposite
sex without the slightest emotion. Still fewer are so
other-worldly that the sight of face or form doesn't
interest them at all.

Most of us have battles to face in this area, battles
with thoughts we are ashamed of, battles that are
fiercer when we are young and before we are married.
But these battles don't end for most of us until we
die.

SOURCES OF TEMPTATION

1. The Tempter

Jesus Christ clearly identified a supernatural personality who approached Him during His forty days of
fasting in the Judean wilderness on the eve of His
three-years public ministry. He called him 'the
tempter' as well as 'the devil' or 'false accuser' or
'Satan'. As He was without human companions or
observers when He was being tempted, we can know
for sure that the Gospel writers are giving us His own
version of the experience. If you read Matthew chapter

4, verses 1-11 you will find that Christ was tempted to become distrustful of His Father's care, and to indulge in a speedy gratification of His natural appetite. He was also tempted to presume on His Father's mercy, and give a sensational proof of divine protection, as well as being tempted to agree with the devil's mishandling of the Old Testament. Perhaps this may warn us against seeking some sensational experience as evidence of a genuine close relationship with God.

Christ was also tempted to secret religious compromise, to give to the devil in private what belonged to God alone. Syncretism has a great appeal in our days! Christ resisted each temptation with a proper use of Scripture, defending Himself with the sword of the Spirit, which is the Word of God.

The same tempter who had been successful in trapping the first human being, Adam, was decisively defeated by our Lord Jesus Christ. Because He never gave way for one moment to the tempter's fiercest or most subtle pressure, He alone qualified to lift us all up by His death and resurrection into a totally new life in which victory over temptation becomes a real possibility for us. 'Because He himself has suffered when He was tempted, He is able to help or succour (run to the help of) those who are being tempted' (See Hebrews 2:18 and contrast with Genesis 3.)

The devil is one of the main sources of temptation, and we must recognise the reality of this supernatural personality and also the reality of his satellite hosts. The New Testament describes these as 'principalities and powers and wicked spirits in heavenly places, the world rulers of this darkness' (Eph.6:12). The devil is called by Christ 'the prince of this world', and by Paul, 'the god of this age' (See John 14:30 and II Cor. 4:4.) And we are all urged to resist him, with all his wiles and claims (See I Peter 5:8,9.)

2. Our own fallen human nature

This is something the Lord Jesus never had. He took
from the Virgin Mary all that He needed of our
humanity to be truly human, without the sin. But even
in the best of us there is enough rebelliousness and
unpleasantness in the heart to be able to account for all
the evil and harm we do, without any need to refer
to satanic interference or demonic influence, or talk
about answers of prayers to Satan offered by followers
of the 'Black Arts'. We must not flatter ourselves that
all our troubles are due to the direct personal intervention of the devil or his hosts! This self-centred
human nature of ours is the root of all the troubles in
society. Society is only man blown up big.

3. The world around us.

Certain shows, plays, films, magazines, paperbacks,
newspapers, advertisements, pin-ups, and sensuous
music all play their part in assailing our minds with
temptations of various kinds. One of the sad facts of
life is that there are those who set about the systematic
brain-washing of others, generally younger than themselves, to lower their moral standards. Haven't you
heard the argument, 'Just think of the relief and help
you could give to that person by a little adultery!'?
There are many influences to get people into the social
drinking habit, and generally lower our resistance to all
sorts of temptations. We must be careful about the
company we keep, as well as about the things we look
at. We are all influenced by others, whether we realise
it or not. We must set our hearts steadfastly against sin,
or sin will dominate our hearts, however outwardly
respectable we may still appear to be. That determination is an important part of the answer to temptation.

THE ANSWER TO TEMPTATION

1. A right relationship with God

We cannot know anything about a life in which we are daily overcoming temptation until we have come into a right relationship with God through Jesus Christ. (See Romans, chapters 3, 5 and 6.) To believe in Christ is more than to believe about Him. It involves trusting Him implicitly, no strings attached, being willing to obey Him daily. Only when the Spirit of God has taken the Word of God and brought to life our dead spirit, so that we become real children of God, can we know a life that is strongly resistant to temptation. It may also mean more temptations than ever before, some of them of a kind never experienced before we became real Christians!

2. Daily Bible reading and prayer

If we start each day reading God's Word and praying to Him, we shall find we are stronger to resist temptation, as surely as day follows dawn. But if we neglect our relationship with God, and unconsciously rely on our own strength to do what is right, we will fail, perhaps badly, no matter how long we have been Christians. Our eyes must ever be on the Lord, the Christ of the Scriptures. We must run our lives constantly looking away from our own resources to Jesus, the Author and Perfector of faith: your faith, my faith. David said, 'I have hidden Your word in my heart, so that I might not sin against You.' (See Hebrews 12:1,2 and Ps. 119:11.)

The words which God has inspired, and which the Holy Spirit lights up and applies to us as we read them daily in humble dependence on the God who gave them, have an insulating as well as an illuminating effect on our minds. The Bible will keep us from sin when God is using it to instruct us and protect us. And we can count on the Holy Spirit to bring to our mind the relevant word in the hour of temptation, just as He did in our Lord's temptations. (See Matthew 4:4,7,10 and Ephesians 6:16,17.) The tempter's siren voice doesn't get through nearly so effectively when we are listening daily and eagerly to our Lord's voice speaking to us through the Bible. We may know for sure that if we do not listen to our Master's voice we will be much more vulnerable to temptation.

As we pray honestly and believingly to God each day we may be sure of getting His help in every time of need, and finding His mercy in every time of failure, as He promised. (See Hebrews 4:15,16.)

3. A frank assessment of our own weaknesses

We are not perfect, even the most mature of us. And none of us is beyond the reach of temptation. One person is left cold by some temptations that nearly tear another person to shreds. We all have different temperaments and backgrounds. We are all in different environments. And we need to discover our particular areas of weakness, which may well vary at different stages of life, e.g. self-sufficiency and uncurbed ambition in youth, often with criticism of older people who 'ought to know better by their age': self-righteousness in middle years, and self-pity in advancing years: 'Nobody loves me anymore!' or, 'I'm completely useless, a drag on the rest of the family!' Knowing ourselves helps us to pin-point these areas of weakness and to have a campaign against the temptations that take advantage of these vulnerable flanks. If you think you have gone out of range of a certain temptation, whatever it is, watch out! Those who think they are no longer at risk, always standing firm, need to be very careful that they don't fail. (See I Corinthians

10:12 cf 13.)

Keeping up-to-date accounts with God is so important. A back-log of failure can be so depressing. 'What's the use of starting to confess? The list is unending. I don't know where to begin.' Keep it on a daily basis. Then it will not be so difficult. Sometimes this confession must be to others as well as to God, if we have wronged someone in some matter that has come between us. Most men seem to find it difficult to say 'sorry': to admit to others that they have been wrong or done wrong. We may feel it is mostly the other person's fault. But we have an obligation to live at peace with everybody as far as we possibly can. We have to work hard at maintaining good relationships. (See Matthew 5:23,24 and Romans 12:18.)

Confessing to God and man when necessary (not forgetting the apologies due so often to one's wife) brings us the relief of forgiveness and cleansing from stains, and the repairing of upset relationships. It also strengthens us to withstand the next temptation. Cleansing brings not only peace: it brings strength. God's cleansing isn't cheap. It cost God the death of His Son on the Cross to make it possible for Him to forgive our sins without lowering His standards, and make it possible for us to withstand temptation in His strength. 'If we claim to be without sin we deceive ourselves, and the truth is not in us. But if we confess our sins God is faithful and just and He will forgive us our sins and cleanse us from all unrighteousness' (I John 1:8,9).

4. Fellowship with Christians

Christians cannot really live successfully and fruitfully on their own, even if there are times when they despair of nearly all the Christians they know! We need each other. We owe it to Christ and to one another to help each other. 'You can tell a man by the company he keeps' is an old proverb and a true one. David, who wrote so many of the Psalms in the Bible, said 'I am a companion of all those who fear You, and of those who keep Your precepts'. We must spur one another on in the fight against temptation, the fight for practical holiness, and we must encourage one another in a life of love and good deeds. Warm Christian fellowship is a great strengthening against temptation, and should make us feel 'I must not let my brothers and sisters down. They are praying for me. I am praying for them. I must not yield to temptation.'

Sharing frankly our personal needs with a close Christian friend can be a great help to withstanding temptation. A married couple or close friends are ready-made units for sharing. But apart from our husband-wife relationship let us be careful to avoid emotional involvement and possible embarrassment. 'Two are better than one...the one will support his companion or fellow-pilgrim' (Ecclesiastes 4:9-12). Christian workers receive many confidences. They need to be doubly careful.

5. Resisting the devil

Some people make too much of the devil. They blame him for everything that goes wrong in their daily lives. They shrug off human responsibility far too easily. They see demons in every illness. Others go to the opposite extreme when they fail to recognise the devil at all in human affairs.

The Bible describes the devil as our enemy, Satan, the false accuser, and pictures him coming to us in two very different guises — sometimes as a 'roaring lion', sometimes as an 'angel of light'. We need to watch out for his subtle approaches. He is always seeking to lead men and women away from God's will for their lives.

He tries to blind us to our own sinfulness and deep need of Christ. He tries to stop us humbling ourselves to come to Christ for forgiveness. He seeks to neutralize us, to divert us from serving Christ with our lives, or else he seeks to goad us into being super-spiritual and neglecting ourselves or our home and family. He is always trying to divide true Christians from one another by exaggerating the importance of secondary things, or by making us feel (stupidly!) 'they did that deliberately to hurt us'.

We are commanded to recognise the reality of the devil and to resist him, standing firm in our faith every day (I Pet. 5:8,9; Rev. 12:9-11). Christians often have to pray, 'Lord Jesus, please come between Satan and me right now'.

6. Steering clear of known sources of temptation

Anything that we know has weakened our resistance to sin in the past calls for radical treatment. If it's a picture, take it down now! Put something beautiful in its place, so that when you look at it you have wholesome thoughts! If it's a play that lowers resistance to sin or makes evil seem attractive, turn off the knob, or refuse to go and see it, as the case may be. Don't dilly-dally if you want victory. It's no use praying each day, 'Lead us not into temptation' if we are careless about contact with what we know will weaken us. God calls us to fill our minds with lovely, admirable, praiseworthy things (Phil. 4:8).

Sometimes the only answer to a particular temptation is to get out of a situation. A strong emotional involvement may even call for a radical change of job and address. Some men with good prospects have had to change their job or at least their department because of an infatuation, an obsession, or the fear of their own will weakening. Far better honourable and timely departure than eventual capitulation to persistent pressure.

This is no new problem. In Pharoah's Egypt long ago, Joseph's youthfulness, good looks and upright bearing were just too attractive for the often-absent-Potiphar's scheming wife. The more she saw of him, the more she became infatuated with her husband's young assistant, with his delightful foreign accent and polite way of speaking. Day after day she tried to break down his resistance to her female charm and alluring scents and desire to have him in her embrace. For his master's sake, for his honour's sake, for her sake, and above all for God's sake, he said 'no' again and again. But like many of her modern counterparts, she wouldn't take 'no' for an answer.

She saw her chance one day when no-one else was in the house. She grabbed his robe and said, seductively, 'Come on, lie with me'. He could see only one way of safety. Flight! Fast! He left his robe in her hand and got out. The frustrated female screamed. She spat out terrible lies about him. And Joseph was not the last to prove that someone's unsatisfied lust and thwarted plans can quickly turn to hate. But God will take care of those who seek to do what is right in His sight. Do you remember the scripture that played such a vital role in the life of Eric Liddell as seen in 'Chariots of Fire'? 'Those that honour Me I will honour', says the Lord. You can read the full exciting story in Genesis chapters 39 to 41.

7. Fixing our eyes upon Christ and His promises

It is possible for mature Christians as well as for beginners (and even in the holiest of environments) to find unholy thoughts or pictures flashing through their mind. If this happens, we must switch our mind deliberately to thinking of Christ hanging on the Cross for us and our sins. This can be a wonderful antidote to many other forms of temptation.

> *Turn your eyes upon Jesus,*
> *Look full in His wonderful face*
> *And the things of earth will grow strangely dim*
> *In the light of His glory and grace.*
> *(Helen Lemmel)*

Another antidote is to take hold of specific promises in the Bible. One that helped me greatly as a student is, 'My eyes are ever on the Lord, for only He will release my feet from the snare' of temptation (Ps.25:15). This is 'the secret of the Lord' which I learned the first time I went to the Keswick Convention. Think of other promises like 'Jesus...shall save His people from their sins'. And 'if the Son shall set you free, you shall be free indeed' (Matt. 1:21; John 8:36).

Often we find a promise in our daily Bible reading that we can turn into prayer. Hang on to God's promises. Whoever else may fail us, God will stand by His word. No temptation has come our way that no-one else has ever faced before. And God is faithful. He will not allow us to be tempted beyond what we can bear. But when we are tempted He will provide a way out, a way of escape (I Cor. 10:13). We can count on Him to keep His word at all costs. Why not tell Him at the start of the day, 'Lord, I don't know all the temptations that are going to hit me today, but I'm looking to You for deliverance'. Then, when temptation strikes, we can shoot up a 'rocket' prayer: 'Lord, help me now'. We can trust Him to answer that prayer.

8. Being alert for Christ's return

We don't want Him to find us in a ghastly mess or ashamed of a particular situation or relationship at His appearing. We cannot know precisely when He will return, but it could be soon. So let us put aside anything we are ashamed of, and cultivate what we know is good for our spiritual life. God's Word tells us to behave decently, not to get involved in orgies and drunkenness — and the drink flows so freely at some parties these days! Sexual immorality (easier to fall into when people have been drinking), debauchery, dissention and jealousy have to be avoided like the plague. Instead, we are to clothe ourselves, as it were, with the Lord Jesus Christ, and not to spend time planning how to gratify the desires of our sinful nature (Romans 13:10-14).

9. Submitting ourselves to God's will for our lives

God loves us so much He wants us to have the very best. And the Bible continually assures us of His love for His children, and His concern for our daily lives. He knows what the future holds for each one of us, joys and sorrows, temptations and testings; and we can trust Him to see us safely Home. We can call upon Him in the day of trouble and know that He will deliver us at the best moment (Psalm 50:15). We can pray something like this:

'Lord Jesus, I am not my own. I am bought with Your blood. Help me to say 'no' to my selfish desires, and 'yes' to all Your will today.'

This is following the Lord's prescription to take our cross daily, deny ourselves daily, and follow Him (Luke 9:23).

Submitting ourselves to God's will does not reduce us to pliable plasticine, easily shaped, with no resistance left. There is a battle to be fought. Christians are called to be good soldiers of Jesus Christ, fighting bravely against temptation. The person who gives him or herself completely to Jesus Christ each day may be tempted more fiercely at times than a compromising, easy-going Christian, because he or she goes on resisting right through to the point of victory. Our Master never calls us to tread a pathway He has not trodden Himself. Nor does He call us to walk alone. He will never leave us, or forsake us (Matthew 26:39; Hebrews 13:5,6).

TEMPTATION AND TESTING

Does it seem rather confusing that temptation is mentioned in the Bible with two quite different meanings? It can mean a temptation to do wrong, which is what we have been considering so far. But it can also mean a testing, which may have no connection with evil, but has to do with the strengthening of faith and the development of character. There is a link between the two, but they are different.

In the New Testament James summarises the distinction like this: When tempted, no-one should say, 'God is tempting me. For God cannot be tempted by evil, nor does He tempt anyone (i.e. attractively suggest to them that they should do what they know to be wrong); but each is tempted when, by his own evil desire, he is dragged away and enticed. Then, after desire (lust in the Authorised Version) has conceived, it gives birth to sin; and sin, when it is full grown, gives birth to death' (James 1:13,14). God may test our faith, e.g. Job, while Satan may tempt us to sin, e.g. Judas.

THE VALUE OF TEMPTATION

We may ask, 'Does temptation serve any useful purpose? Has it any positive value?' Yes, indeed! Just as physical muscles are made stronger through meeting resistance, so our spiritual fibre is made stronger through resisting temptation.

There is much wisdom in the old hymn:

Yield not to temptation, for yielding is sin;
Each victory will help you some other to win;
Fight manfully onward, dark passions subdue,
Look ever to Jesus, He will carry you through.

Shun evil companions, bad language disdain,
God's name hold in reverence, nor take it in vain;
Be thoughtful and earnest, kind-hearted and true,
Look ever to Jesus, He will carry you through.

To him who overcomes now, God will give a crown,
Through faith we shall conquer, tho' often cast down;
He who is our Saviour our strength will renew;
Look ever to Jesus, He will carry you through.

Ask the Saviour to help you,
Comfort, strengthen and keep you;
He is willing to save you,
He will carry you through.

(H.R. Palmer)

Each time we overcome temptation, we become stronger in the battle against sin. And the sight of Christians not weakening under pressure encourages younger ones to stand against sin and for the Faith. Another great value of temptation is that experiencing it creates sympathy for others who feel its pull. The person who has never been tempted in a certain way may find it hard to sympathize with or encourage those who face a similar temptation.

Those who have faced and overcome the temptation to use the Lord's day for their own pleasure in organised games, or academic work or music, are best equipped to help those facing this temptation. Christians who have learned to be scrupulously honest in business are those who can help most the young people who are facing all the temptations of today's business world, with its fierce competitive spirit.

Those who have learned to live without unnecessary luxuries can, by their example, help others to fight the unending battle against covetousness and materialism.

Most Christians recoil from the whole idea of homosexual practices. Those who have felt and fought the inborn tendencies (which are not in themselves sinful) are best equipped to help to put iron into the will of those tempted towards a homosexual relationship, sinful in God's eyes (Romans 1:26,27).

Only those tempted to lose patience with difficult in-laws can bring the utmost sympathy and understanding to those facing similar problems. Only those physically handicapped, tempted to feel they were given a raw deal compared with some of their vigorously active friends, can bring the deepest sympathy to those similarly tempted.

One reason why our Saviour Christ took our humanity was that in all points He might be tempted as we are. With His perfectly genuine human nature at God's right hand, He remembers, and feels for us in our infirmities, weaknesses, and temptations. With His equally genuine Divine nature, as truly God as He is truly Man, sharing the throne of Godhead with His Father, He is able to rescue us in the hour of temptation (Hebrews 2:18; 4:14-16; 7:25-27).

So we may sum up by saying that Christ Himself, delivering us, is the great Answer to temptation.

The Saviour rose in victory
O'er the hosts of the evil one,
The Saviour lives to share with me
All the triumphs He has won;
Then no more need I fearful be,

Or Christian conflict shun,
For the Lord most High gives even me
The Victory of His Son'.

(E.H.G. Sargent)

By His sacrificial death He has made atonement for all our sinfulness: sins of omission (things we have left undone which we ought to have done), and sins of commission (things we have done which we ought not to have done) (Hebrews 10:12; 9:24-28).

And by His endless life, full of tender concern for us and power to rescue us, He is able to deliver us when we are tempted (Hebrews 2:18; 7:25). As we keep close to Christ, we keep on top of temptation. But sinfulness and the capacity and tendency to fall remain in us as long as we are on this earth (I John 1:7-10). Mercifully, God as Judge looks on His children as covered with the perfections and beauty and sinlessness of Christ. But God as our loving heavenly Father is perfectly aware of our weakness, and does not want us to wear blinkers about our weaknesses. For it is only when we are aware of our weakness that we cling tightly to Christ and His promises, leaning on His promises to us, not on ours to Him.

The risen, conquering Christ is the answer to your temptations and mine. Once He has got hold of us, He will not let go of us, in spite of our struggles, weaknesses, and failures, until He has brought us safely Home, either at our death or at His second coming.

Christ's words to Paul are His words to us: 'My grace is sufficient for you. My power is made perfect in weakness' (II Corinthians 12:9,10).

When I fear my faith will fail,
Christ will hold me fast.

When the tempter would prevail,
Christ will hold me fast.

For my Saviour loves me so
He will hold me fast.

　　　　　　　　　　(Ada Habershon)

Chapter 9

HAPPY MARRIAGE

The Institution of Marriage (Matthew 19:4-6)

The Pharisees had faced the Lord Jesus with a loaded question about divorce. He made no reference in His reply to the authority of the famous Rabbi Hillel, who had made divorce easy, or to Rabbi Shammai, who only permitted it on the ground of adultery. He referred only to the authority of the Word of God through Moses. For whereas He knew that the Mosaic ceremonies would shortly be changed, and the New Covenant based on His unique sacrifice at Calvary would very soon replace the Old, He would have us know that God's moral standards are unchanging for all generations.

The God behind creation is the God who made the distinction between male and female, with a view to the union of husband and wife. In His purpose we find separation as well as union: 'For this cause shall a man leave father and mother.' The marriage relationship takes precedence over that between parents and children. None of us choose our parents, though many of us may feel we could not possibly have done better if the choice had been left in our hands. Only one Person in history chose His mother, and that was the Lord Jesus Christ Himself.

In the same purpose of God there is to be unswervingly loyal adhesion of husband to wife at all times. The husband is to cleave to his wife and she to him, as long as they both shall live. Divorce has never been in the purpose of God. In His plan marriage is for life, and divorce was permitted by God's servant Moses only because of the hardness of men's hearts. God planned that a married couple should stay together 'for better, for worse, for richer, for poorer', till death. Only adultery (v.9) or wilful desertion (I Cor. 7:15) entitles an injured spouse as a very last resort to claim the freedom of divorce according to the permitting Scriptures.

Divorce is always an evil, but occasionally it is the least of several possible evils, especially in the interest of children suffering in a home where the atmosphere is appalling and behaviour flouts all the laws of love. But the planning Scriptures all point to marriage as a permanency.

This introduces a solemnity and a sacredness that overrides all other human bonds. Marriage is absolutely unique. In the Biblical mathematics of this subject one plus one equals one, not two! 'The twain (two) shall be one flesh.' It is a terrible thing to come between husband and wife. Some people excuse themselves on the ground that the couple were not ideally suited to one another and were already drifting apart. But the part of a true friend is to help the couple to come closer together, not to drive them further apart. As in all moral issues, two blacks don't make a white. To edge out a lawful spouse is wanton sin, utterly inexcusable. This sort of sin on a large scale has led to the crumbling of great empires.

THE BASIS OF CHRISTIAN MARRIAGE

Christians should form and hold the highest ideals of marriage. Christian young people should take the utmost care only to marry in the will of God and to build their homes on a secure basis. Christian marriage begins in the heart of God. 'Marriage is honourable in all, and the bed undefiled' (Heb. 13:4). Chastity, so important before marriage, continues within the sacred bond of marriage. There is no impurity in divinely ordained marriage.

True Christian marriage can only exist where the two parties have both come to the foot of the cross and found Jesus Christ as their personal Saviour. And true Christian marriage starts in prayer. Ideally, each should be praying about their partner long before they meet. Prayer before marriage as well as throughout married life is a wonderful investment in heaven's bank.

Is marriage for all? No! But the unmarried woman who is in the centre of the will of God is much happier than she would have been if she had 'hooked a man', out of God's will. From my limited observation, I would say without hesitation that the woman who is unhappily married experiences far more emotional strain and tension than the most lonely unmarried woman. God knows what is best for each of His children, and we must learn to trust Him about this. Very few remain unmarried all their lives, but some of the Christian women who remain single can testify that the Lord Jesus has given them wonderful peace and joy. He does satisfy the longing soul.

SOME SECRETS OF HAPPY MARRIAGE

(1) Christ first

Put Christ first and your partner next. To put your husband or wife first and Christ second will not bring deep and lasting happiness, because it is not the way God planned for us.

Charles Alexander's life motto was 'Only one day at a time to live, only one Person to please'. And he didn't mean Mrs. Alexander! But to seek to please the Lord Jesus was to please Mrs. Alexander. She was the right kind of Christian wife. He did not feel worthy of her, nor she of him. And that is how it should be.

(2) Mutual sharing

Christian couples should share everything – business, finance, interests, thoughts, opinions, temptations, fears, joys and all the in-between feelings. Open your hearts completely and utterly to each other. Fusion of heart means fulness of peace in the home, when there is no conscious barrier between you both and the Lord.

(2) Prayerfulness

When a husband and wife start the day with prayer, both separately and together, the day is started on the right footing. Many Christian couples would testify to the enormous difference it makes to pray about the details of their united lives. One of the best things an engaged couple can do is to start the habit of praying together whenever they can. This will then be a natural part of their relationship when they are married. Those who pray together stay together.

(4) Courtesy and appreciation

Don't take each other for granted. Husband, watch her hands. Don't let her do work that is too heavy for her. Watch her eyes, and try to stop her over-doing things before she reaches breaking-point. See that you nourish and cherish her as you once promised. Wife, don't nag him when he comes home tired. Remember he likes to see you looking nice, and, if you do, he is more likely to speak that word of appreciation you long to hear!

Some husbands treat their wives just like the washing-machine or dish-washer. They watched their wife's eyes eagerly in the earlier, romantic days, but they seldom observe with compassion and understanding the tiredness that comes with the hard work of the home. A mother with young children works a sixteen-hour day!

Are you more polite to someone else's wife (husband) than you are to your own? If so, you are robbing each other of pleasure and the peace of a gracious home, and your children of a good example. Words of courtesy and appreciation cost so little and mean so much. Expensive flowers produced for anniversaries cannot possibly make up for neglected daily courtesies.

(5) Unselfishness

If you are to enjoy to the full the richness of Christian marriage you must die daily to self and self-interest and live to Christ. See that thanksgiving is a frequent note in your prayers. Cultivate the daily bearing of one another's burdens, and the daily forbearing from blurting out the unkind word you will sometimes be tempted to say.

Let your partner see that you are utterly faithful, honouring your vows. Let it be known that your wife has your steadfast allegiance. This adds to her stability and poise, her sense of security and the aura of serenity that marks a happily married woman. You owe her far more than you dream!

The world needs more genuinely Christian marriages and happy Christian homes. If we are married, let us pray that our partnership may be more glorifying to God. But if we are not married yet let us pray we shall marry only in the will of God. (See Ps. 84:11.)

(6) Take care

Marriage is not a panacea for all emotional ills, though happy marriage is an enormous safeguard against wrong sexual liaisons. To use a simple analogy, the man who has had a really good meal at a respectable restaurant or hotel or friend's home is not tempted to go in for the fish and chips he can smell as he passes the shop on his way home! To be more explicit, the man who has a really good relationship, including regular intercourse (more important to most men than it seems to be to most women), is not nearly so vulnerable as the man who has a poor relationship with the woman he has married. Hence the old saying, 'Marry in haste, repent at leisure'. How much care we must take to see we really 'mesh' mentally, spiritually and emotionally, as well as culturally, before we take the plunge!

(7) Guarding against unfaithfulness

A Christian minister had an early morning call from some friends in another town: 'My husband has committed adultery. Will you please talk to him?' The wife felt rejected, polluted, hurt beyond words. How had it come to this pass? Quite simply. He had felt it his duty to counsel and try to comfort a woman about his wife's age when her husband ditched her. Eager to help, he put his arms around the poor, distraught woman. This brought her great comfort. She really liked it. He found he did too. And instead of passing her on to his wife for further counselling, the next thing was the chemistry which exists between a man and a woman took over. And they were away, both of them experiencing the sexual exhilaration they had felt long years earlier with their lawful partners. It was not too long before they were in bed together. Then came discovery, the moment of truth. And the man who had made promises to the second woman, who kept telling him how wonderful he was, and what a marvellous father he would be to her nearly grown-up children (never mind his own), had to weigh up these promises against the vows he had made to his wife in the sight of God and many of the Lord's people. He now had to hurt one of the two women very deeply indeed by breaking with her. Ghastly dilemma. In God's mercy he has honoured afresh the vows he had broken in his passion. He is back with his wife, who has forgiven him, and is seeking to be all that a woman could need from a man. The fire of their early romantic days has been rekindled. But the memory of the hurt will linger long. And the other woman was both angry and frustrated, and quite sure that her need of this man's presence, comfort and love is greater than his wife's need, because she reckons the wife is a stronger person than she is. How easily we can deceive ourselves.

Where did things go wrong? In the first instance, husband and wife, after twenty-five years or so of living together, had settled down into what might be described as a good business relationship. They had allowed the fires of romance to die down, if not go out altogether. He was not making time for her. He had lost sight of Christ's example of sacrificial love, referred to by Paul in the context of the husband-wife relationship in Ephesians chapter 5, verse 21 to the end.

(8) Some questions for husbands who care

Does the element of self-sacifice enter into my thinking about my wife? Or does she always have to fit into my plans, my ideas of what our duty is, my thoughts (if any!) about using leisure time? Must she come to watch cricket, football or tennis just because I like it? Does she have to look at the box so much in the winter, stifling domestic and intelligent conversation? Does she always have to go where I want? Or not go somewhere attractive to her just because I don't particularly want to go there, or think I'm too tired?

Does she look increasingly harassed, or increasingly joyful, indeed radiant?

Do I always look up and smile welcomingly when she comes into the room? Do our eyes meet often? Magic moments!

Am I reading the Bible with her and leading her to the Throne of Grace, preferably at the start and end of each day?

Am I doing all I can to see that she has a Quiet Time some time during the day? Or am I jealous of the time she spends alone with God?

Do I look after the breakfast, and perhaps the evening meal too, at least one day a week? Or do I reckon that's her job, and she must do it on her own? I suppose there are still some very old-fashioned husbands left! I take my hat off to the average husband of today.

Do I mark off in my diary at least one evening a week for my wife, for us to be together or to do things together?

Am I backing her up loyally in her handling of the children? Am I leaving all the disciplining to her? Am I a soft touch with the children , rather to her disappointment?

Am I quick to praise her, for her appearance, for her cooking, for her house-keeping? Do I still tell her how beautiful she is to me, even if her standard reply is, 'What nonsense!'?

Do I just walk out of the room and leave her when she's reduced to tears? Or do I wrap my arms around her, and tell her I'm sorry I'm only a man, so I don't understand, but I do love her? Do I tell her how sorry I am for anything I've said or left unsaid which has contributed to her tearfulness? Most men are so slow to say sorry! Am I still making her my best friend? She knows she was the sweetheart of my youth. Have I made her appreciate the fact that she is the closest and cherished companion of my middle years (if I've got there) and will be the dearest friend of my retirement years, ever the darling of my heart? No-one knows me better. No-one understands me better. No-one has had so much to put up with from me! Do I keep telling her how much I appreciate her? She will never weary of hearing this from my lips. Most wives simply glow when their husbands express their appreciation. A little word of appreciation goes a long way towards protecting both her and myself from the fires of romantic love dying down. Without doing any disservice to the Lord's work or the Lord's people, we can remain a courting couple all our days. Even elderly spinsters have told me how much they appreciate seeing couples obviously still in love years after they were married! And those in a steadfast relationship of ongoing love can bring a fresh quality to their Christian service.

Do I link all that is attractive that I see in other women with my wife, determined to cultivate that in her? Or do I allow myself the pitiful luxury of comparing her unfavourably with other women I meet? If so, I must watch out. There is a serpent waiting to spit poison into every beautiful relationship. Whereas those in a steadfast relationship of ongoing love can bring a quality to their Christian service which is sorely needed in these days of great insecurity.

Am I unable to spare the time to go with her when she's looking for a new dress? Do I (on principle!) look disapproving of anything she comes home with when I was too busy to accompany her?

Do I complain about the money she spends on hair-do's?

Do I object to the way she handles the tooth-paste tube, forgetting how much stronger men's hands are?

Am I lost in the newspaper at breakfast?

How many times a day must I listen to the news? Doesn't it matter to me that she finds this an awful bore, and finds me a pretty poor table companion? We don't have to talk all the time, but ears and tongue are better left switched on at the ready! If our marriage is to be at its best, we must learn to rejoice over one another's company, and not to resent it as an intrusion into our private lives! Happy marriage has to be worked hard at, but the rich rewards are simply incalculable. The price is well worth paying! Do I have some apologies to make? Or is thanking God all I need to do?

(9) Divorce

Divorce is doubly tragic when Christians are involved. They are going back on a covenant they made before the living God (Malachi 2:14-16). And it is terribly tragic when there are children, for separating parents are saying loudly to their children, 'When the going gets tough, you just clear out and do your own thing'. None of us should think, 'It couldn't possibly happen to us'. We are all vulnerable. Moving in Christian circles doesn't give us total protection. The chemistry between the sexes is powerful. Too much time spent with an attractive woman can lead to disaster. We don't need to blame prayers uttered to Satan in witches' covens. The inflammable material is all to hand without any covens having a go!

Chapter 10
SINGLENESS, MARRIAGE, AND COURTSHIP

Singleness or marriage?

If you are single, do you enjoy being single? The Lord Jesus was the most perfect man who has ever lived on this earth, and He was single. He was not unfulfilled because He never married or experienced sex. He was the most complete and balanced person the world has ever seen. So we should not be surprised that some of the choicest Christians have remained single all their days. (Even if some of their married friends were inclined to think it was a shame they didn't find a suitable life-partner!)

We must not forget our Lord's words in Matthew 19:12, 'Some are eunuchs because they were born that way; others were made that way by men; and others have renounced marriage because of the kingdom of heaven. The one who can accept this (i.e. who has the gift of celibacy) should accept it.'

The apostle Paul underlines his Master's teaching: 'I would like you to be free from concern. An unmarried man is concerned about the Lord's affairs, how he may please the Lord. But a married man is concerned about the affairs of this world, how he can please his wife, and his interests are divided. An unmarried woman or virgin is concerned about the Lord's affairs. Her aim is to be devoted to the Lord in both body and spirit. But a married woman is concerned about the affairs of this world – how she can please her husband. I am saying this for your own good, not to restrict you, but that you may live in a right way in undivided devotion to the Lord' (I Cor. 7:32-35).

In this same chapter Paul describes singleness as a gift of God, literally a charisma (verse 7). It is evident from the context (verse 26) that the Corinthian church was going through a time of crisis, and this teaching is not Paul's last word on the subject of getting married. Writing some years later to young Timothy, whom he had left at Ephesus to help the infant church there, he says he favours young widows getting married again, bearing children, and looking after their homes well (I Tim. 5:9-14).

It used to be said that single people can more readily offer mobility, and married people hospitality. But I don't think that applies so much these days, when some singles are among the most hospitable and thoughtful of hosts and hostesses. Single people are also usually able to be more flexible with their time, though they have no more of it than anyone else!

Singleness is a state to be enjoyed as one of God's good gifts, to be used for the good of others. So is marriage, which God established at creation (Gen 2:20-24), often called a creation ordinance. The problem many have had to face is, 'How can we know when God is withdrawing the gift of singleness to replace it with the gift of marriage?' It is a fact of life that most people get married sooner or later. This is implied in Genesis 2, where we find that God's remedy for man's aloneness was to provide for him a suitable partner. This remains God's usual remedy for the aloneness of mankind.

Most of us, if we are single as we read this, will at some stage consider the possibility of marriage, if we have not already done so. If we have reached the point of wondering about a particular person as a potential life-partner, here I suggest some questions which are worth asking before we proceed towards a serious relationship of commitment to one another.

TEST QUESTIONS FOR A YOUNG PERSON TO ASK HIMSELF OR HERSELF ABOUT SOMEONE WITH WHOM HE OR SHE IS CONTEMPLATING THE POSSIBILITY OF MARRIAGE

Do we share the same convictions about the Bible, Church, Evangelism, Sundays, Christian service, life-style (e.g. alcohol) etc.?

Can we read and pray together without feeling 'What a waste of time!' or 'I suppose we'd better!'?

Does being with him or her make me want to 'go places' for the Lord, appreciate God's Word more, pray more, live a better life?

Do I feel worthy of him or her? If so, there is something wrong!

Could I cope with seeing this face at the breakfast table every day for the rest of my life?

Does the more I see of him or her make me feel more sure that he or she is the answer to years of prayer, mine and other people's?

Do I admire this person for his or her godliness, or only for good looks, face, image, style, body and added fragrance?

Does he or she make me feel closer to older Christians I admired before, or do they come between us?

Do friends of the same sex share Christian things freely with him or her? Are they eager to see my partner again? What do these friends think of him or her?

Does my partner share me readily, and even proudly (in a humble sort of way!)? Do others feel included when they are with us?

Do people say: 'How well matched you are...You make each other blossom'? Or are they silent, cautious of commending, a bit uneasy?

Is he or she outgoing, friendly, and keen on hospitality, or withdrawn, shy, and a little fearful of meeting too many people, only wanting to be with me all the time? N.B. There are times to be alone.

Do we have lots to talk about when we meet? Is my partners voice 'music to my ears'?

Do we have some practical/cultural interests in common, e.g. sport, music, walking...?

Does he or she appreciate my sense of humour, laughing readily?

What does my family think?

Can we move freely in each other's family circles?

Am I happy for my children to look like, talk like and behave like my partner...and parents?

Do our best friends think this relationship is really good, or do they suspect it's 'only the chemistry'?

CHRISTIAN COURTSHIP

Modern contraception has given women a freedom for sexual relationships no previous century knew. This has led to more casual sex and trial marriages. But both pre-marital sex and trial marriage are 'out' for Christians (I Cor. 6:12-20). Sex belongs to marriage. There should be no sex without the responsibility of life-long, mutual commitment. (In any case the only entirely fool-proof method of contraception is entire abstention!)

If you have decided to marry, here are some HELPFUL HINTS from people who have passed this way before you on the road to happy marriage.

Consider one another's highest interest...Part at a reasonable hour! Don't go on nattering about sweet nothings into the small hours. Be disciplined! Don't hang around one another's necks so late at night that you are stepping up temptation, or are both so tired the next day that you can't give your boss a good day's work.

Consider each other's need of sleep, which may vary

from person to person and from situation to situation.

Don't let this wonderful relationship be badly spoken of! 'Keep your digits off the differences' is a rule many have found very helpful. Keep the things that belong to marriage for the great time when you can give yourselves completely to one another with total abandonment, good conscience and exclusive delight.

Don't forget it is difficult to 'go down a gear' in your expression of love, so discipline yourselves to a sensible tempo in the run-up to marriage. Some who have rushed ahead of a wise expression of love have really felt pain when they had to 'slam on the brakes', and found it difficult to start up smoothly again. Consummation is so well worth waiting for. It is beautiful in God's good time. The Song of Solomon, that marvellous love poem which God has caused to be put in our Bible, speaks of the physical love we have to give as a beautiful garden enclosed by a high wall. We open the door to its delight when we enter the mutual commitment of marriage. Until that day we should not nip over the wall and prematurely pick some of the 'love apples'. Unripe fruit can have a very bitter taste – and we harm one another by lack of mutual respect. Do lots of things together, like decorating, gardening, helping the parents when you can.

Never forget that younger eyes are on you. Give them a good example. You can make them feel, 'This is good. The more I see of these two, the more I like what I see', or you can put them off the whole idea of courtship and marriage!

Don't be so exclusive that your other friends feel totally neglected, even if they say very graciously that they understand perfectly! It is good when your friends can say, 'They still have time for me. Their relationship is not so exclusive that no-one can get near them these days without feeling an intruder'.

If the relationship is right in the sight of God, and is proceeding at a pace that pleases Him, you will both be nicer to live with, wherever you are. A wholesome relationship will have beneficial consequences all round, far from making you a dead loss to society in general!

Finally, read all the good books you can lay your hands on to prepare you for what is the most important change in your life and life-style.

Chapter 11

RULES FOR THE
CHRISTIAN LIFE?

'I wish there was a rule for everything,' he said wistfully. 'Then I would know where I was. As it is, I am often completely foxed. Please tell me what I ought to do.'

A rule for everything? Would you like to have a rule for everything? Maybe you didn't know that the Pharisees in our Lord's day had a rule for everything. They had rules about eating and washing, rules about what they should wear and what they should do with their money, and literally hundreds of detailed rules concerning the Sabbath Day. You didn't have to think through any situation. You just looked in the book of rules, or, easier still, asked a scribe what the book said you should do!

What did our Lord think about this? The Gospels make it quite clear that He viewed it as something abhorrent to God, something that made hypocrisy easier and true religion not only harder but impossible. Don't forget it was to a Pharisee that the well-known words about the necessity for a completely new birth were first addressed. The Pharisees were dealing punctiliously with petty details and turning a blind eye to the things that really mattered. They made a great fuss about putting aside for the temple an exact tithe of every little thing they grew in their gardens. But they neglected the obvious duties of being fair (justice) and showing mercy and being honest. The Lord called them blind guides because they were leading those who followed them on a pathway to spiritual disaster. He said they were, as it were, straining out tiny gnats, for fear of taking something 'unclean' into their bodies, and yet swallowing camels, ignoring things that brought great defilement to mind and conscience.

All these rules and regulations had come between the individual and God. They were all part of a misleading window-dressing that made it look to the casual observer as if everything within must be splendid. And the Lord made it quite clear that He had no time for this sort of thing. (See Matt. 23:23-28.) He steadfastly upheld the Ten Commandments His Father had given through Moses. But He equally steadfastly opposed the massive addition of rules made by the Pharisees. He held no brief for religious advisers who built their client's faith and life on rules for particular cases and kept these clients in a state of constant dependence on them for the correct advice, instead of introducing them to broad, general principles to be applied in individual situations.

Yes, they had a rule for everything! And it tended towards superficial, religious activity which left no room for freedom of spirit and personal communion with the living God Himself. All their time and energy went into trying to keep the rules. Perhaps you are glad that there isn't a rule for everything in the Christian life! But are there no rules at all? Indeed, there are — most important rules and great principles.

The greatest rule of all is, 'You shall love the Lord your God with all your heart, and with all your soul, and with all your mind, and with all your strength' (Mark 12:30). A man's emotional, religious and intellectual capacities, and his physical powers, too, must all be used for the glory of the living God. There is no real love where there is no real self-giving. All that we have and are must be yielded to God's will for our lives and not to our own selfish pleasure and the furtherance of our self-centred ambitions.

'I am guilty of the greatest sin in the world!' a young man said to me. He had just realised that, if the first and greatest commandment is to love God with all the heart and soul and mind and strength, then to break this commandment is to be guilty of the first and greatest sin. And what was true of this young man is true of us all.

Merely to agree with this gets us nowhere. Right on the threshold of the Christian life is the rule about repentance. Our Lord has laid down most emphatically that a man must repent of his sins, and particularly of his critical and independent attitude towards God, or he cannot begin to live the Christian life. The rebel must be reconciled. This is a basic rule, which applies to progress in the Christian life as well as entrance into it. Unconfessed and unforsaken sin in the life of a Christian robs many a believer of the joy of Christian living.

Alongside repentance must come faith in the Lord Jesus Christ, trusting Him to do for us what we cannot do for ourselves. It is only when we come to Him in repentance and faith that we can begin to love God with all our heart and soul and mind and strength.

Moving from our duty to God to our duty to man, we find what our Lord called 'the second' commandment, to love our neighbour as ourselves (Mark 12:31), carried to an even higher plane in John 13:34, 'Love one another, as I have loved you.' The rabbis' teaching on the second commandment got as far as: 'Don't do to somebody else what you would not like them to do to you.' Our Lord makes this more positive and demanding: 'Do to others what you would like them to do to you.' When we obey this rule of love in genuine, outgoing acts of kindness and attitudes of unselfishness and thoughtfulness we will find we are keeping the remaining commandments of the decalogue. 'Love is the fulfilling of the law' (Rom. 13:10).

In the New Testament we find two outstanding fresh commandments coming from the lips of the Lord Jesus Christ. He said, 'Do this in remembrance of Me', with reference to taking bread and wine as a memorial of His suffering for our sins. This is a Christian rule which we cannot lightly neglect without impoverishing ourselves spiritually. And 'Preach the gospel to every creature' is a rule binding upon all Christians, not just upon the apostles, because the promise attached to it extends to the end of the age.

There are also many unchanging principles in the New Testament to be applied to changing situations through the centuries of the Christian Church. These principles will always be in harmony with the rules, for Scripture is a united whole. We will consider a few of them.

WOULD THIS PLEASE THE LORD JESUS?
(II Timothy 2:4; Romans 15:1-3)

If I love Him I will want to do what pleases Him and to avoid the things I consider would grieve Him. If the Bible anywhere condemns what I am thinking of doing, e.g. a close relationship like marriage with an unbeliever, then I know it cannot please Him. I have no right to do just what I like in the light of the price He paid for me (I Cor. 6:19,20).

WOULD I BE HAPPY FOR HIM TO COME AND FIND ME DOING THIS?
(Luke 12:43)

To ask ourselves this question can often decide the issue.

'Right, my dear, I'll buy three tickets.'

'Three tickets! What on earth do you want three

tickets for?'

'One for our unseen Companion, the Lord Jesus.'

'But He wouldn't go to a show like this.'

'Then, don't you think we ought to stay away to please Him?'

John Wesley was given some sound advice by his mother when he was at Oxford.

'Whatever weakens your reason, impairs the tenderness of your conscience, obscures your sense of God or takes off the relish for spiritual things, whatever increases the authority of your body over your mind, that thing for you is sin.'

WILL THIS STUMBLE A YOUNGER CHRISTIAN?
(See Romans 14)

The power of example and influence is often stronger than we think, especially upon young people. Something we can do without ill effect upon ourselves, because we are older or stronger, may have disastrous effects upon a younger or weaker person. We must therefore consider the effects of our actions on others. Many of us thank God for some particularly gracious and godly life that has stirred up our desire to live a similar life.

Last, but by no means least,

WILL THIS STRENGTHEN MY FELLOW-CHRISTIANS?
(Romans 14; I Corinthians 10:31-33)

We are meant to build up our fellow believers, not to burden them with our failures. A builder or a burden? Which are you? Which are you going to be? People can so quickly form impressions, rightly or wrongly, of churches, or Christian unions or groups, by their acquaintance with just one member. What impression do you give to those who know you? Are they drawn to your Saviour or repelled? Each of us has our part to play. May we live so close to our Lord Jesus that we truly glorify Him.

Chapter 12

UNANSWERED PRAYER

Are you troubled because your prayers do not seem to be answered? I was once speaking on the first part of John 15:16. At the end of the meeting a lady came up to me and said, 'I had so hoped you would go on to the second part of the verse.' She went on to tell me that in her experience it didn't seem to work. The things she asked for did not come her way. The circumstances she asked for did not slot into place.

Have you been feeling there does not seem to be much point in going on? Before you lose all your enthusiasm for prayer, ask yourself these questions:

(1) Have I ever been really definite, regular, systematic about prayer?

(2) Have I ever realised that God's great enemy is Satan, who will do his utmost to hinder me from praying?

(3) Has it dawned on me that there is a natural disinclination to pray that assails all Christians at times and has to be fought with determination, and that prayer habits have to be formed and maintained if I am not to drift into self-reliance, with or without outward religious observances?

(4) Is my basic problem that I am not a Christian at all, and that I cannot reasonably expect to have the Heavenly Father's ear for my affairs yet because I have not yet become His son or daughter by putting my faith in Christ Jesus?

ARE YOU SURE YOUR PRAYERS ARE NOT ANSWERED?

Sometimes we misunderstand the very nature of an answer. 'Yes' is not the only answer to a request. A child asking for a chocolate biscuit just before a meal is almost certain to be told, 'No, dear; it would take away your appetite for what will do you much more good.' That child is not entitled to complain, 'Mummy doesn't love me; she didn't give me what I asked for.' For 'No' is also an answer, even if it is not the answer we would like for our personal comfort or short-sighted preference.

As a child, Amy Carmichael prayed very earnestly and hopefully one night that God would change the colour of her eyes from brown to blue. When she climbed a chair to look in the mirror the next morning her faith in prayer was somewhat rocked, until she remembered that 'No' is an answer! Years later, in India, Amy Carmichael learned to thank God that her eyes were brown. Indian children used to climb readily on to her lap, taking to her immediately, partly because they sensed her deep love for them and partly because her eyes were brown, just like theirs, and they felt she belonged to them.

Perhaps you feel your prayers are about much more important things and that only a little child would pray a prayer like that. But the principle remains that God's foreseeing wisdom may allow some things to be unchanged because He knows the future.

'Yes' and 'No' are not the only possible answers to prayer. 'Yes, but not your way,' is a third. Sometimes we pray for someone's physical healing. Those who believe sickness can never be in the permissive will of God pray with complete confidence for healing and incline to blame the sufferer's lack of faith if they do not recover. But those who seek God's sovereignty in this matter remember His answer to Paul's prayer for the removal of a physical trial. 'My grace is sufficient for thee.' The New Testament mentions the illness of various Christians without any hint that they were lacking in faith or had stepped aside from the will of God.

A Christian leader whose wife had just died wrote in a personal letter, 'For a time I had to pray in the consciousness that God's power was still able to heal, then there came the quiet realisation that, whilst the power was there, His purpose was otherwise...I think her last words to me were: "Ask the Lord to take me home..." We cannot imagine the extreme weariness of the body in those last hours and the longing of the spirit to be homing Godwards...The whole (funeral) service will radiate the joy of the risen Lord. The Christian Church has done far too little to make such services triumphant occasions of our faith.'

God can heal anybody of any disease. God can do it through means or without means. God can heal when the medical world can do no more for a patient, but this does not mean He will or must do so for the asking. By all means let us pray for the recovery of the sick, so long as we preface our prayers by, 'If it be Your will...' But let our prayers concentrate more on the glory of God and the spiritual blessing of the patient and others.

We may have admired the sincerity of the sailor who kept long vigil in front of Sir Winston Churchill's home, praying for that great man's physical recovery. But Scripture, history and common-sense tell us that, apart from Christians alive at Christ's return, death must come to us all, and Sir Winston Churchill had a remarkably long and full life.

Many people, even some Christians, have altogether wrong ideas about prayer. Prayer is not an attempt to change God's mind! Real prayer is communion with

God, expressing our trust in Him, seeking to know His mind on the decisions and situations of life, submitting to His will, resisting in His Name the efforts of the devil to frustrate His loving purposes in human lives.

We must not lose sight of the fact that there are times when we do not understand God's ways. At such times we trust Him implicitly, knowing that one day we shall understand. Years later we may see the purpose of some situation that seemed to be unaltered despite much earnest prayer. Sometimes we shall have to wait till we get to heaven to know the answer to our 'Why?' But we must not falter in our trust in God because of our limited understanding.

A fourth answer is: 'Yes, but not yet.' Some who pray for the restoration of loved ones to mental sanity and perfect balance feel that this is the answer the Lord has given them deep down in their hearts. Others who pray for the conversion of some member of their family feel the same about their prayers. God takes time to humble human pride and bring men to an end of themselves. He does not treat men as puppets. He who is all-powerful and sovereign in the outworking of His purposes in this world in which we live has chosen to respect the will He has given to His creatures, fallen and rebellious though they are. He waits His time, where we in our impatience and fear would rush in and break another's will regardless of whether he can see the truth that is so clear to us. We know from our own experience how slow we ourselves are to pray with utmost sincerity that the Lord will bring us round to do His will at all costs, bending our wills to His, moulding us into the likeness of His Son.

George Muller, that great man of prayer, prayed for sixty years for the conversion of one of his friends. When Muller died, that man was still unconverted. But a few weeks after Muller's death this old man turned to Christ in repentance and faith. George Muller might have felt God was not answering his prayers, but the answer had all the time been: 'Yes, but not yet.'

When we turn to the Bible we find a number of references to prayer not being answered.

The Psalmist speaks of his prayer returning to his own bosom (35:13), or, as some people we know may say, 'My prayer only got as far as the ceiling.'

God says to His backsliding people Israel through His servant Isaiah (1:15), 'When you make many prayers, I will not hear...' Jeremiah complains, 'When I cry...He shuts out my prayer' (Lam. 3:8).

In Daniel 10 we read of Satanic opposition to fervent, believing prayer, the answer to prayer being held up by opposing powers of darkness, principalities and powers arrayed against God's purposes and therefore against His servant (vs. 10-14, cf. Eph. 6:10-12).

And in John 11 we read of the divine overruling of fervent, believing prayer. The answer to the prayer of Mary and Martha for healing was delayed because the Lord purposed to do something better for them than they asked. 'The glory of God' (John 11:3,40) does not figure largely enough in our prayers. May God help us to learn to pray that, whatever else may or may not happen, He will get the glory and honour due to His great Name in the situations we bring before Him. And things can happen, when His glory is the supreme aim of our prayers, which are hindered from happening when our own comfort, joy and convenience, or even the blessing of others, hold too large a place in our thinking. God grant us a deep, genuine concern for His glory, which will affect all our thinking and all our praying. When we have this, no part of our life will be unaffected. We will live our lives on a higher plane, as well as entering into new depths of prayer communion.

Chapter 13

IS CHRISTIANITY
THE ONLY WAY?

'You don't mean to tell me you believe that Christianity is the only way? How can you be so narrow-minded?' The questioner sounded at least disappointed if not a trifle impatient with his Christian friend.

No normal person likes to be thought narrow-minded. But the Christian realised that what his friend thought of him personally was not nearly so important as what he thought about the Christian faith. So he answered:

'It all depends on what you mean by Christianity and what you mean by "way". That word "way" can be used in more than one sense; and much that passes for Christianity has little in common with the Christianity of the New Testament.'

His friend replied, 'But whatever you mean by "way", surely all religions lead to God. After all, it is sincerity that counts most. It doesn't really matter what you believe so long as you are sincere.'

What was the Christian to say to this very popular argument, with its idea of everybody being all right in the end? His reply was as frank as it was courteous: 'In some ways I wish I could agree with you. It would be nice to think of everyone getting there in the end, though I can't help wondering just how far lawlessness might go if everyone believed that! But I am a Christian, with a first-hand experience of Christianity. And since I became a Christian, I have become certain that the Bible is God's Word and that its teaching is therefore completely trustworthy. And the Bible makes it quite clear that Jesus Christ is the only way to God. Jesus didn't say, "I am a way to God"; He said, "I am the way, the truth, and the life; no man comes to the Father, except by Me."

'In my own experience,' the Christian went on, 'I have found Him to be the way to God. It took infinitely more than sincerity and effort on my part to bring me to God. It took something which only God could do, and He did it through Christ. You may say this is just my subjective experience, but my beliefs are based on objective facts, the historical facts of Christ, and on His unique claims, not on religious theories. If you will take the time and trouble to study His claims for yourself, particularly in John's Gospel, you will find the evidence all points in one direction, that Christ is, in fact, the Son of God and the only way to God.'

Conversations something like this often take place in many parts of the world, wherever Christians are concerned enough to talk about their faith. And what a difference it would make if all Christians were as active as Jehovah Witnesses or Mormons are in spreading their respective faiths!

Sad to say, many professing Christians share the views of non-Christians on the question of all religious roads leading to God. At a worldwide Anglican Congress in Toronto a leading church statesman was reported as saying, 'We should be bold to insist that God was speaking in the cave in the hill outside Mecca; that God brought illumination to the man who once sat under a Bo-tree.' Did he really mean that we should recognise Islam with its sacred Mecca, and Buddhism with its sacred Bo-tree, as authentic revelations of the same living God who spoke through Jesus Christ? Such words can hardly convey any other meaning.

Professor Arnold Toynbee, the world-famous historian, goes further than this in *Reconsiderations* (the twelfth volume of his studies in history). He asserts that the whole idea of incarnation must be rejected as being something unworthy of God. His reason is that any advances made by God to man would need to be made in a universal manner. It is inconceivable to him that God should take human flesh and live in a tiny land on the eastern shores of the Mediterranean. But the burning question is not whether we can imagine such a thing happening but whether, in fact, it did happen.

History books and the Bible alike testify to the fact that Jesus Christ lived in Palestine nearly two thousand years ago. The Bible alone reveals the significance of His life, and those who study its pages with an unprejudiced mind come to the same conclusion as C.S. Lewis, that He was either 'mad, or bad or God'.

The young Christian said, 'It depends on what you mean by "way".' If by 'way' you mean philosophy or way of life, then it is obvious that Christianity is not the only way in that sense. Materialism is a way. Humanism is a way. Communism is a way (even in the 1990's). All the large non-Christian religions of the world represent a way of life. And we must admit that a certain degree of satisfaction is to be found in ways of life other than the Christian way. There are devotees of other faiths and philosophies who seem quite content as they are, although their deepest needs are not met.

Christianity includes a way of life, but it is much more than that; for the heart of Christianity is a personal relationship with Christ Himself. Christ, the eternal Son of God, came from His Father's home to this earth to do for His creatures what they could never do for themselves. He did not come only to show what God is like, though He did this so perfectly that He could say, 'He who has seen Me has seen the Father.' He came to open the way for sinful, selfish people to enter the presence of God. He came to put away the sin and defilement which would otherwise cut us off from

God for ever. God's appointed way for Him to do this was by going bearing the judgement due to sin. The only sinless Man the world has ever known was Himself made sin for us, that we might be made fit for heaven. This, in a nutshell, is the meaning of the cross. Something absolutely awful happened to Him so that something absolutely wonderful might happen to us.

But surely all the other religions of the world are not totally devoid of all truth? No, indeed; they cannot bring you to God, but there are elements of truth in all religions and philosophies. If you are content to seek fragments of spiritual truth you may find them in almost any religion and philosophy in the world. But in Christianity alone you will find the *whole* truth God has revealed about Himself.

If you listen to the pundits of other faiths, read their sacred books, attend their worship (where it is public), observe their devotees, what will you find? Sometimes deep sincerity, sometimes sheer formalism; on some faces, signs of peaceful resignation, on others tokens of restless dissatisfaction or even blank despair. But you search in vain for the things so distinctive of true Christianity.

Christianity is unique in at least these respects:

(1) It is the only faith in the world that offers the forgiveness of sins here and now at the expense of the life of its Founder.

(2) It is the only faith in the world that offers a direct personal relationship with the Founder of the faith.

(3) It is the only faith in the world that offers eternal life as a free gift here on earth to start the believer off on his heavenly pilgrimage, rather than as a goal or prize at journey's end.

(4) All other faiths allow or encourage you to bring something to God for your acceptance with Him. But Christianity allows you to bring nothing but your sin.

(5) All other faiths are based on the principle of man seeking after God. But Christianity is essentially God seeking after man.

(6) Christianity alone gives all the glory to God in the way a man is made fit for heaven.

(7) Christianity alone meets the basic needs of human nature, giving to those who come to Christ in repentance and faith the things they need most – forgiveness, peace of mind, assurance about the future, purpose in life.

Some readers may still be a little uneasy about the exclusive claims of Christianity and feel that so long as people of other religions are sincere and devout, that is all that matters. Does the wrong train get you to the right place so long as you believe sincerely that you are on the right train? Will poison taken from a bottle in the dark do you no harm so long as you sincerely believe you are taking the medicine the doctor prescribed? It is right to have a high regard for sincerity and to dislike humbug and hypocrisy. But we need truth as well as sincerity, facts as well as faith.

Many people think that tolerance is the chief moral virtue and that intolerance is an almost unforgiveable sin. But a dogmatic man who knows what he is talking about is more help than a tolerant man who is unaware of danger. God's Word speaks of judgement to come, and of Christ as the only way of safety. It is well to take God at His word.

A surgeon once said to a patient, 'You have a small growth and we would like you to come into hospital for up to six days for its removal.' This did not stir up resentment in the patient; it brought relief. Had he said, 'You have a small growth and you are fortunate to have come to the only surgeon who can deal with it,' this would have aroused considerable surprise or even resentment, when there are so many skilled surgeons in the world. On the other hand, it might have been true! New methods of treatment are constantly being found, and occasionally one particular surgeon pioneers the way for a time until others follow suit. Christ's treatment is unique. He is still operating on the souls of men. He can cope with us all. He needs no successors, though He has countless assistants throughout the world. But it goes against the grain to believe that Christ alone can deal with the cancer of sin. It is only when we experience His working in our hearts and come to realise who He is that we can believe His claim to be the only way must be true. All over the world there are those who have tried to find God by other ways, and they searched in vain, until they turned to Christ.

A devout Hindu woman visited a school for the blind, run by Christians in India. 'They have no light in their eyes,' she said, 'but they have light in their hearts. I have light in my eyes, but I have no light in my heart.'

May those of us who have found light and life in Christ share our knowledge with others who need Him every bit as much. 'There is salvation in no-one else, for there is no other name under heaven given among men by which we must be saved' (Acts 4:12 R.S.V.).

Bible
Guidelines
by
Derek Prime

Teachings from the Bible

about
The Ten Commandments

The Fruit of the Spirit

Commitment to Christ

and

other areas of vital importance

Useful for personal or group Bible study.

Derek Prime is a well-known conference speaker and author

224 pages   *pocket paperback*

Christian Warfare
And Armour

by
James Philip

An exposition of Paul's description of the conflict between believers and Satan.

An exhortation to stand fast in the Lord.

An encouragement to fight until the victory is won.

James Philip is minister of Holyrood Abbey Church of Scotland, Edinburgh.

113pp   *pocket paperback*

The
Growing Christian

James Philip

If we belong to Christ we should be maturing in our Christian faith.

Previously published as 'Christian Maturity'.

96pp   *pocket paperback*

The
Spurgeon
Collection

The Saint and His Saviour

Till He Come

Faith

The King's Highway

Around the Wicket Gate

John Ploughman's Talks

John Ploughman's Pictures

Come Ye Children

All of Grace

Christ's Glorious Achievements

Other volumes to follow

Books

available from

Christian Focus Publications

Geanies House

Fearn, Ross-shire

write for our current catalogue